Inkirragat to me. Uobreta to an age-mate intimate. Sammy to European and American acquaintances. This is Sekerot Ole Mpetti, Maasai, in whom are found all the good things of his race. What I was to learn about the people of Maa and Africa, he graciously and patiently taught me.

This is where my spirit had always been. Where my body had never set foot, but where all of me belonged.

A
TENT
WITH
A VIEW

An Intimate African Experience

ROBERT VAVRA

William Morrow & Company, Inc.
New York

For Muv, for everything . . .

Library of Congress Cataloging-in-Publication Data

Vavra, Robert.
    A tent with a view : an intimate African experience / Robert Vavra.
        p.   cm.
    ISBN 0-688-09890-8
    1. Natural history—Kenya. 2. Vavra, Robert—Journeys—Kenya. 3. Kenya—
Description and travel. I. Title.
QH195.K4V42 1991
508.6762—dc20

91-7556
CIP

Printed in Spain

First Edition

1 2 3 4 5 6 7 8 9 10

Printed in Spain by Cayfosa, Barcelona

Photographic laboratory associate, Rick Fabares

Design by the author

"Can you hear *Loneliness*?" asked Sekerot, pointing to the canopy of an umbrella acacia. "Maasai call the cicada *Eliyio,* or 'Loneliness' because she sings sadly in her tree until we walk under it, then becomes contentedly silent in our company."

And so it was with me. In the presence of Africa, my loneliness at last was quiet.

For five weeks in the summer of 1989, not another white face—except my own in a cracked mirror—would darken the camp, which was in the hills that rise to the southeast above Maasai Mara. There, I would be gifted with an opportunity that few men enjoy: to live out, in middle age, childhood fantasies. Our days would have no plan. There would be no cardboard, familiar conversation. The only words that would reach my ears would come from Maasai lips. We would keep no schedule, would have no routine, except that which nature imposed on us

for eating and sleeping. My friend Sekerot Ole Mpetti, who had made the adventure possible, and I would roam the Kenyan Highlands on foot or on horseback, light-years from anything that had been contaminated by "civilization."

As a child, books about Africa had veiled my imagination in wonderment. Though I would later live in Spain, always at the back of my mind would be southwestern Kenya. But as time passed and each year I sadly read of the approaching extinction of yet another East African animal, equally worrisome was the fear that perhaps the Kenya of Ernest Hemingway, Martin and Osa Johnson, Carl Akeley and Karen Blixen had been irreversibly polluted by tourists and sterilized by scientists doing behavioral studies. Like the late Myles Turner, former warden of the Serengeti, I was disturbed by the vision of acacia panoramas dominated by zebra-striped minivans and lions wearing fluorescent-red, radio-tracking collars. Might it not be better to stay home in Spain, to travel to 7

Africa only by way of imagination, and keep alive forever the romance that had existed in me beyond memory?

In 1984 I met Dr. William Felix Wheeler at a book signing in San Diego where he introduced himself and spoke to me of his adventures. During the last eight years he had traveled over thirty thousand miles by camel with the Tuaregs across the Sahara, on foot accompanied by pygmies in Zaire, but mostly in a Land-Rover called the Elm Tree, which he maintained in Kenya. From the time of that initial meeting, year after year when I returned to America, Bill Wheeler expressed the same intensity about Africa until finally, in 1988, he convinced me to accompany him on safari.

During that first trip to Kenya, the Africa that from childhood I had worshipped had been disappointing and illusive, except for a three-day foot safari into the Loita Hills. Before those short but glorious "Loita days," we were restricted in the game parks to the Land-Rover and had been unable to smell the country, masked from us by gas fumes, prevented from hearing it by the motor's roar, and separated from earth and plants—that most basic of experience—by the vehicle floorboards. Also, my two American companions on that adventure were, innocently, almost a constant reminder of the white Western world from which I had sought temporary asylum. They sang country blues songs and strummed flamenco on the guitar as we roared past tourist lodges which streamed with pale-face comfort and acrylic khaki. Here were New Jersey telephone operators, factory workers from Liverpool, and Tokyo bank tellers, none of whom would have been in Africa had modern convenience not made it so affordable and facile. Acapulco would have held like appeal, except here, instead of wearing flowered shirts and straw sombreros, they dressed as if for some Halloween safari theme party.

Zebra-striped minivans full of these spectators (almost gone are the days of *travelers*), like vultures, flocked around any lion kill. Elephant and rhino, long accustomed to the presence of man, stood placidly while being photographed from all angles and with every possible lens, as nonthreatening as if they had been safely penned up in the Bronx Zoo. Absolutely no interest was shown in my favorite, the Cape buffalo, about which Laurens van der Post wrote: "Much as I love the lion, elephant, kudu and eland, the animal closest to the earth and with most of the quintessence of Africa in its being is for me the buffalo of the serene marble brow."

The Africa of zebra-striped minivans was not that written about by Akeley, the Johnsons, Blixen, van der Post, Hemingway, and Markham. Their adored words described a world where it seemed my spirit had always been, where my body had never set foot, but where all of me belonged. Most of the Maasai we had met on that 1988 trip, long tarnished by tourists, like Tijuana beggars, held out their hands for a coin in exchange for being photographed, or tried to hard-sell their beaded wares. Where were the proud, noble people of *West with the Night* and *Out of Africa*?

During that first trip, on the day when we abandoned the Land-Rover, far from the reserves, and strode into the Loita Hills with six Maasai porters, we felt we were stepping from some glitzy, mediocre, late-night television travelogue and into the glorious, adrenaline-rushing Africa of all those boyhood dreams. Our destination was Naiminenkiyio, the Forest of the Lost Child, and the Nguruman escarpment from which we hoped to see Lake Natron and maybe even Ol Doinyo Lengai. It was then, when still accompanied by white companions who were less intensely in touch with nature, that I vowed to one day return to the Kenyan Highlands, avoiding reserves, with only Africa—its wildlife and native people—for a companion.

(continued on page 162)

8

A TENT WITH A VIEW

Ololasurai, meaning "place of the serpent," was

the seemingly uninviting name for an isolated

valley in the low hills above Maasai Mara. Sekerot

took me there with the promise of a campsite

The plain below Ololasurai was a constant parade of

stomping hooves, a pageant of horn, stripes, and spots,

exotically marked and tinted, yet subtle to the eye. There

were great phalanxes and endless files of migrating

wildebeest, whose numbers could no more easily be

counted than grains of sand on the shore.

The lightning-scarred fever tree that
stood between the tent and the stream
was named for its proximity to water
and the infirmity it nurtured.

To the left of the tent was a long valley that ended in a wall of mountain eroded and pitted with caves now inhabited by a band of Ndorobo hunters. The morning of my arrival they had made a kill. A bull giraffe had risen to watch the dawn, not knowing it would be his last.

During the six months before we arrived, lions had

reportedly eaten five humans near Ololasurai. One of

my horses would also lose her life to them.

Each morning as the tent flap was drawn, it was as though the curtain of a theater had risen. But the drama that daily unfolded outside had neither a script nor a guaranteed conclusion.

Morkau was of the Purko clan. At Ololasurai he

would be my spear, my eyes and ears, the shadow

on my trail.

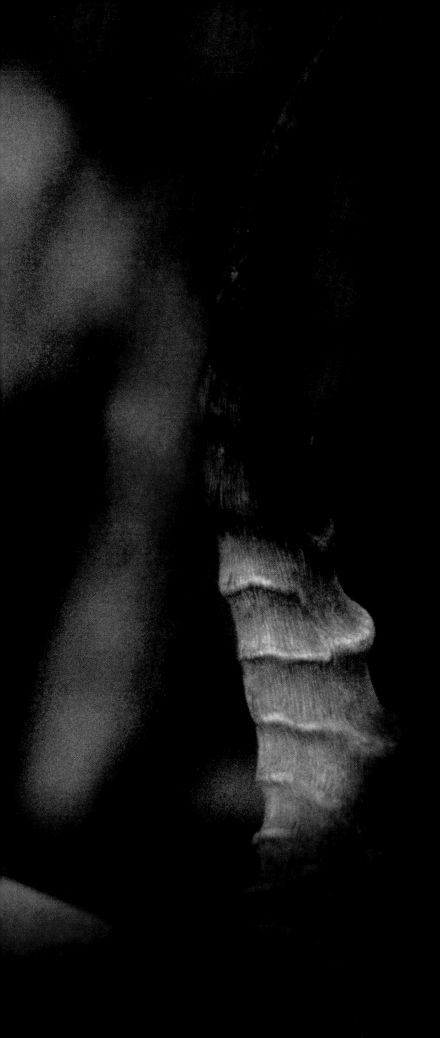

This is Sikona. The blade of his spear would know the blood of the lion who tried to harm our horses.

Often I was left in camp with Sameri, Sekerot's

delightful twelve-year-old reed of a brother, who

fortunately was still too young to find constant

translation boring. It was both amusing and

attractive to hear my own thoughts expressed in his

sweet voice and in words I could not understand.

Lepish was also of the Purko clan. Elephants and buffalo he had hunted as at camp he would hunt our laughter with his jokes. He would light our smiles as he lit our fire.

Moseka came from beyond the Sand River—from

Tanzania. His words would quiet our mares as

would his touch. At the campfire, years spent with

grazing cattle would be described in song to us by

his high boy's voice, which in lion-like grunts

would also tell of warrior days.

One afternoon the smell of rain was in the air when a Maasai

appeared against the darkening sky. Like others who had

passed by the tent, he was sure to be scouting fresh grazing

Green had returned to the hills of Africa. Fire, combined with water, had brought good grazing to Ololasurai, and the people of Maa were moving toward the tent. They came from the plains, the hills—from out of the past. In the days and weeks that followed, it seemed that few passed by, or raised temporary corrals and shelter in the valley, without visiting camp.

Smiles and laughter were often dimmed

when someone arrived to tell us that echoed

barking heard the night before was all that

remained after a predator had carried off a

sheep, goat, cow, or even the dog who had

guarded them.

As the people of Maa passed by the tent, Sekerot

convinced them to pose for me. The rainfly and our

camp became a studio. The sky provided lighting;

bright yellow grass or the green canvas, reflectors; leaves

and branches, filters; the forest and hills, backdrops.

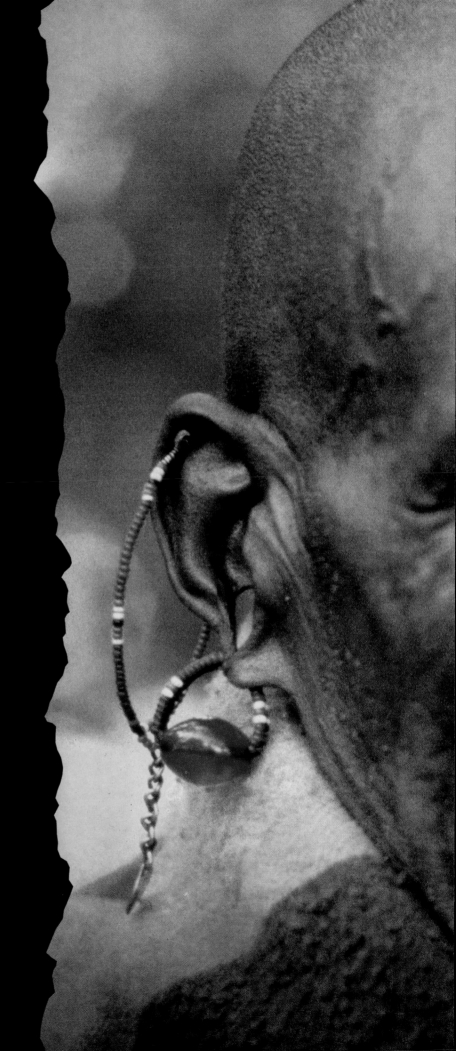

Soon I became acquainted with some of the herdsmen who daily visited our camp. Those like Turere, Ntiti, Kardasha, and Rereu seemed to enjoy our company and spent hours sitting on the grass or logs outside of the tent.

As the days passed, even the intensity of our photographic

sessions could not distract from my first African passion,

Cape buffalo. Overlooked, degraded, and dismissed by

tourists as dull and cow-like, Cape buffalo have stirred special

feelings in certain men, among them Hemingway, Michener,

and van der Post.

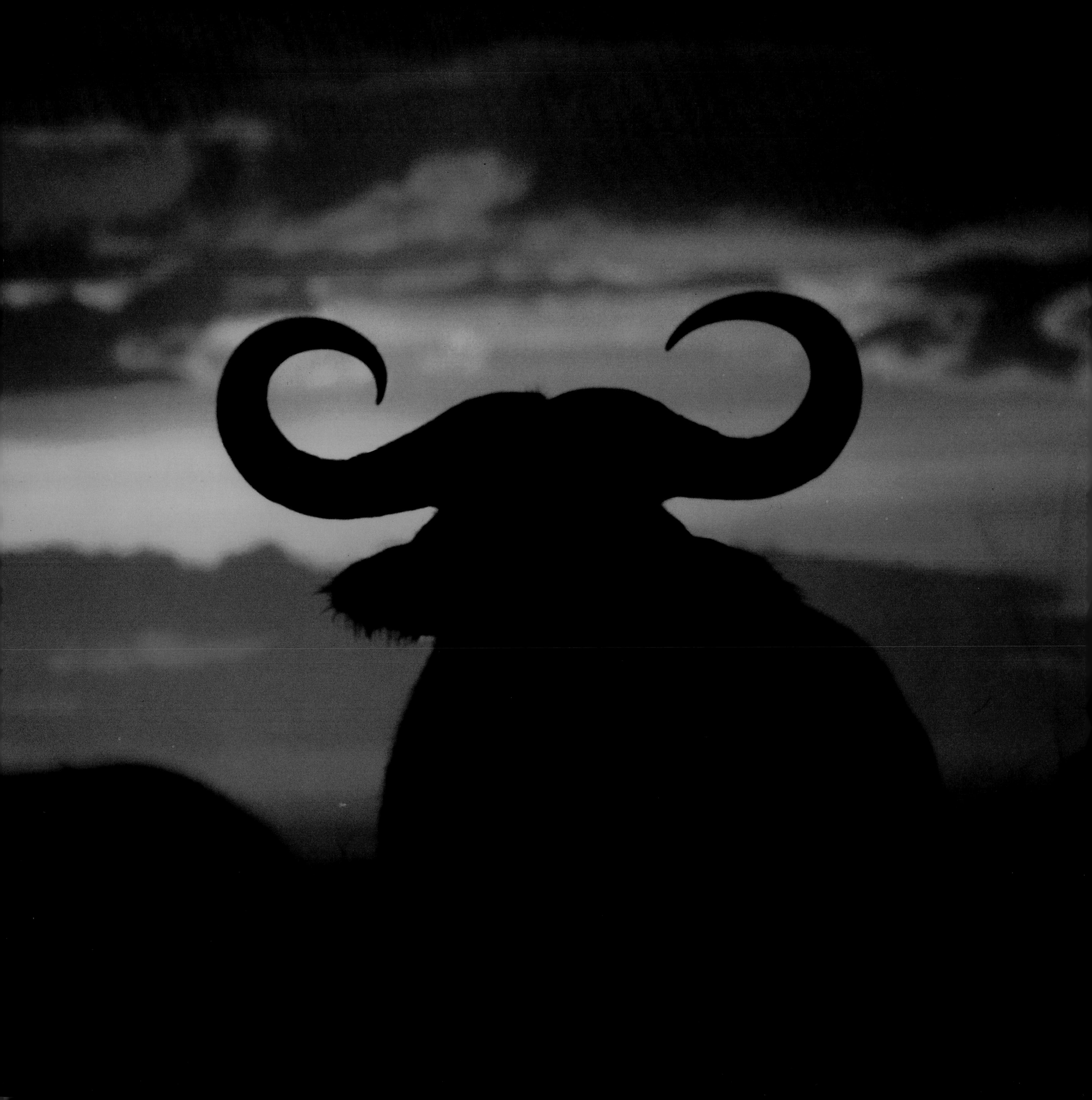

marks they left in the mud or the nests they bent in grass on the hillside—did not come within daytime view of the tent, we would send two former warriors in search of them.

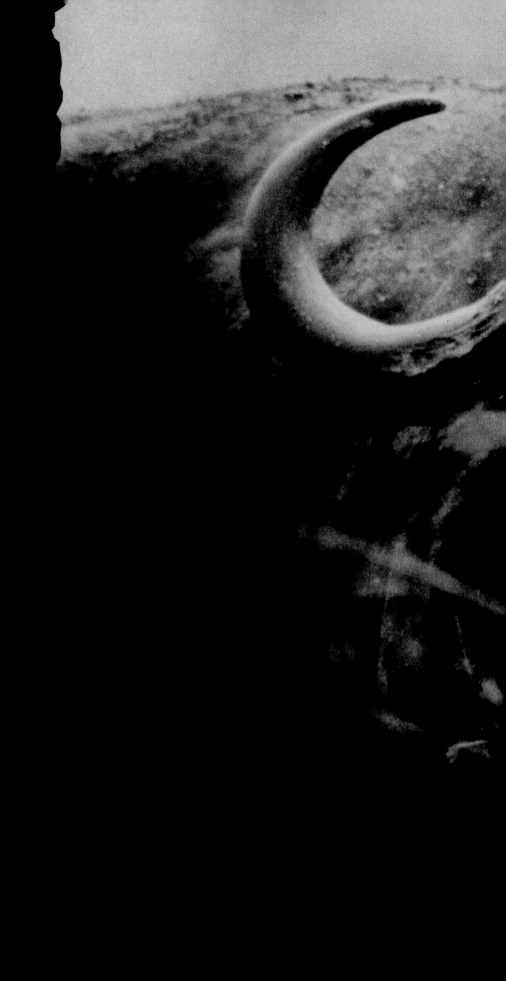

As with Africa itself, I sensed with the buffalo

death as companion. These feelings, in part, came

with the memory of a foot safari into the Loita

Hills where I had leapt from a tree to face a raging

bull, which was seconds from goring and bashing

a friend from existence. That nightmarish

experience would forever change the lives of the

three of us who had barely survived it.

Away from the tourist routes the Maasai that I had previously seen had been

distant, exotic figures, like wild animals spontaneously captured by a camera in

documentary images. The Maasai who came to us were people with basic

human emotions and responses—like us, but ornamented with beads and

ochers, evocative coiffures, and armed with spears, short swords, and clubs,

while framed within what seemed the most attractive of landscapes.

How could anyone, Hemingway and Blixen included,

be disappointed with the view from the tent with which

Sekerot had provided me? To this setting, the mares,

Katie and Narok, arrived like half-expected lottery

prizes. Horse odors, neighs, and nickers added another

perspective to the camp, and I found fraternity and

peace in their presence as I have in the company of

equines everywhere.

Adding to the eeriness: a seal pup with

The life of women, while subservient as well as restricted, is somewhat less complicated than that of the Maasai male. Their dark beauty around camp was seldom seen but much anticipated.

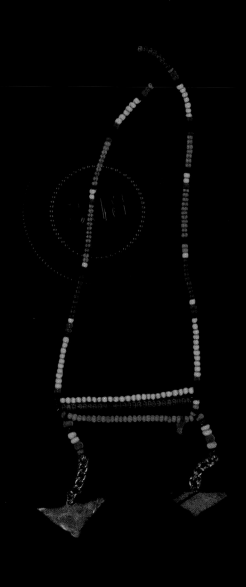

It took a lion or leopard far less effort to leap a thorn fence, where night after night they were assured of finding a meal, than casting the hillsides in quest of antelope which had the whole of Ololasurai in which to escape.

Maasai boys sometimes sat or stood around the table near the stream where I typed, giggling as I pounded out in caps, ink on paper, names which were theirs but which most of them could neither read nor relate to their identity.

Making our way toward camp, if lions announced

their presence downstream or near the caves, I

stopped to savor the noise, much to Sameri's

Ntiti's smile, voice, and manner

brought brightness to camp even when

clouds marbled the sky.

. . . the people who visited the tent, though

they might have questioned and been

confused about other topics, were

unconsciously and absolutely certain of one

thing: who they were—Maasai.

Night after night, when we were in bed and the fire no more than a trace of orange, Chui would jump camp and dash through the darkness to his enkang home a half mile upstream. Anyone who knows about leopards and dogs will find it unbelievable that this yellow flash in the blackness repeated his seemingly suicidal run for thirty-one nights. In the end, it was not a leopard, but an immature lion, that ended both our pet's nightime sojourns and his life.

One afternoon an unusual golden light fell

on all that lay outside the tent. For a few

seconds a dark figure appeared against this

scene and was gone. I took it to be Kardasha

who, among the youths who visited camp,

seemed most to represent the prototype of the

Maasai pre-warrior, the boy on the edge of

manhood.

Once free of the stream's saplings and tangles, my heels touched the black mare into canter. Zebra galloped off, angling to gaze back at us. Impala fled in soaring leaps. Topi stampeded by, rouge-slate flashes through a lattice of thorn, and ahead, giraffe loped from the horizon more as if to escape the rising sun than us.

In the faces of some Maasai matriarchs could be read the tale of a

people whose iron code of tradition not only makes them unique

among the earth's beings but has allowed them to prevail in a

corrupting, hostile, almost overpoweringly seductive white man's

world.

Frequently I would awaken from a siesta to find Morkau waiting quietly outside the tent, hoping that his presence would be requested on an afternoon walk. Most camp chores were acts that Maasai machismo had excluded from the lives of the men who came to work for us. Yet our friends mastered those tasks with accomplishment and acceptance, and without complaint. However, a chance to stroll the hills with me was for them like a vacation from school.

Sekerot's body was as fast as that of a cobra,

and so was his mind. Also, it seemed that his

heart was totally unfamiliar with the word

"fear." What I was to learn about the people

of Maa and Africa, he graciously and

patiently taught me.

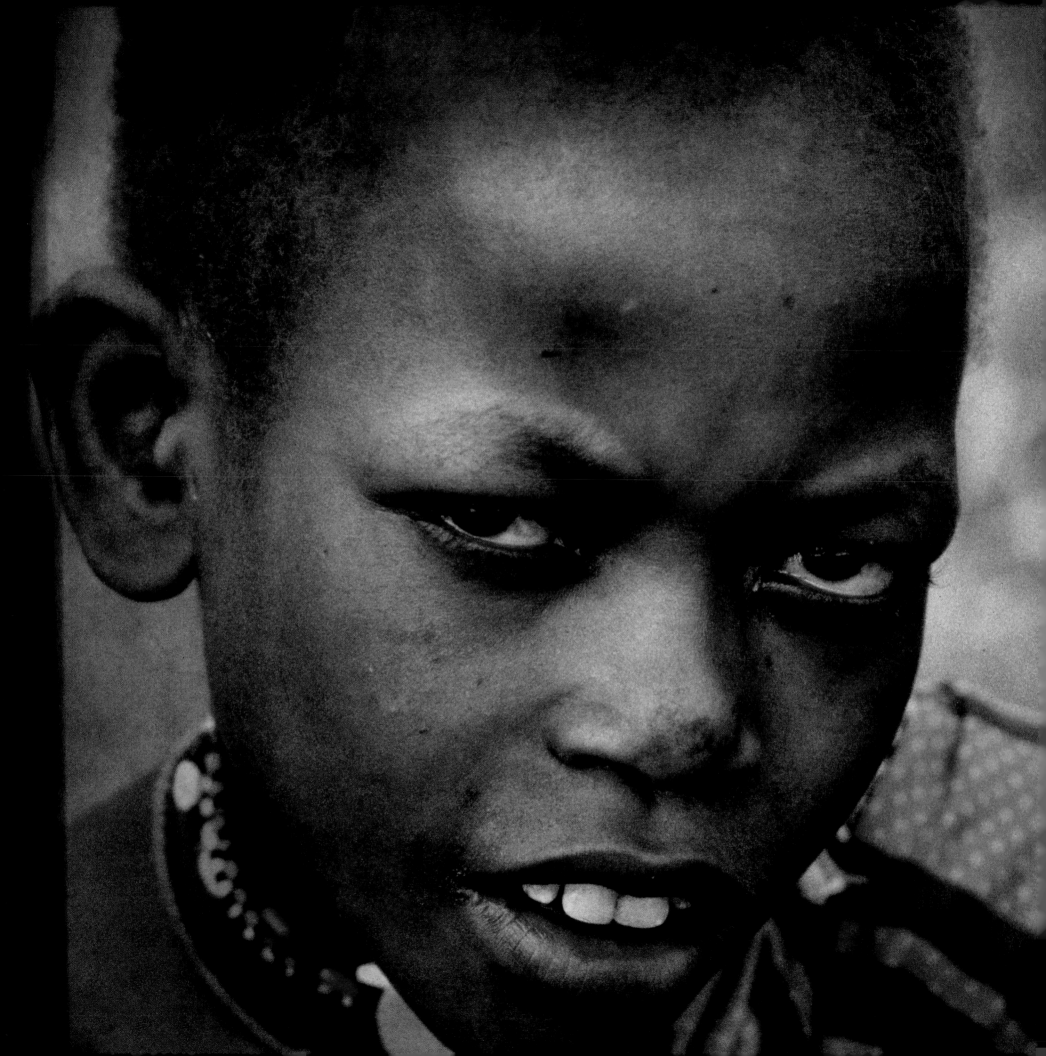

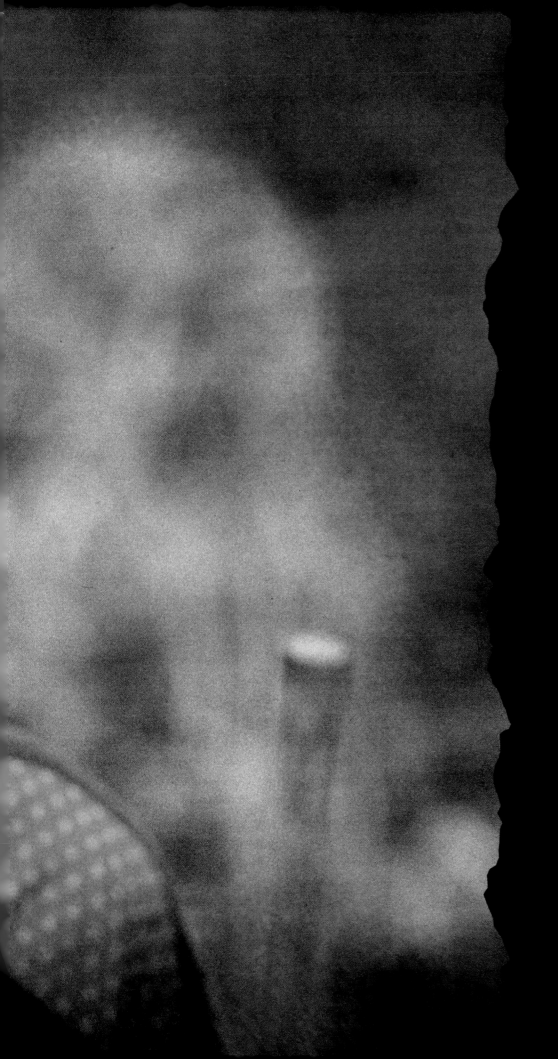

The boy could not have been more than

eight but he was one of those children cursed

with the face of an old man. Accompanying

his aspect was a shrewd and cunning

character, shown again and again by the

hard bargains he forced when being paid for

chores around camp.

Upstream from the tent, the water changed color to that of flowing

lava, reflecting the red canopy of wait-a-bit thorn trees, whose

branches at dusk were shaken by baboons which peered

menacingly.

The countenance of the Maasai

aged is etched with a past which

was as insular as it is seemingly

romantic. The future that can be

read in the eyes of their

grandchildren is not only

nebulous but unpromising.

Finally, as if scheduled, the rains did come every afternoon between three and five, cumulus gathering above the mountains to the east, while beyond the camp the sky darkened. In minutes, the black cotton soil would be drenched and water was eddying around the earth platform upon which the tent had been wisely set.

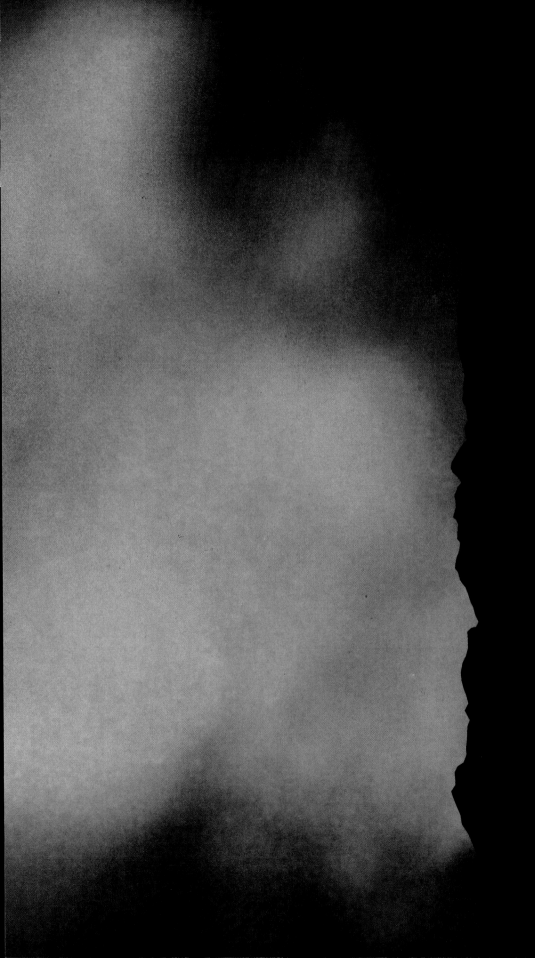

For hours I would sit on a log or stretch out on the grass, totally happy in the company of my new Maasai companions. I was as curious about the wild animals that affected their daily lives as they were mystified by a white man who took such an interest in their world. Frequently as they bade good-bye, they said to Sameri, "Tell him thank you for respecting us and our conversation." These words, heard again and again, were enough to rouse feelings from a stone.

When I took on the responsibility for Kardasha's circumcision

ceremony, I became not only his second father but symbolically the

husband to his mother, which caused good-natured joking

whenever I arrived at their enkang, three hours' walk from camp.

One girl of particular dark and sulky beauty

seemed to enjoy visiting our camp and often

brought us milk or yogurt. Infrequently, when a

changing mood or joke caused her to smile, the

day became especially joyful at Ololasurai.

How different was this place where all children bow

their heads respectfully to receive an adult's

condescending but affectionate touch.

Midday often blew hot breath to cast a

saffron pall over this hill where zebra

stomped the charred ground, pluming their

hooves in eruptions of ash while calling in

voices more like those of yapping lapdogs

than of the earth's most exotic equines.

At first maybe, like other whites before me, I

chose to believe the Maasai something they were

not, like falling in love with persons for the way

they appear, not the way they are, looking beyond

a stare to see something where there is nothing.

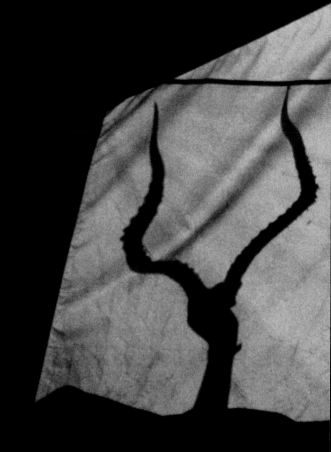

Even before the tent flap was drawn, the view was often

as dramatic as were the rumblings of elephants and cries

of eagles that came from the unseen world outside.

Morkau and Moseka grew to love and call our horses

by name. Unfortunately little time would pass, however,

before lions would return to camp. A scruffy-maned

male was the first to crash through the woven acacia

branches, and before Sicona could spear it in the side,

my favorite mare lay dead with her black neck broken.

How different was this place from anything my

being had previously experienced. Here man lived

in harmony with nature, surrounded by the earth's

most exotic wildlife—the trophy hunter's Valhalla,

home of the "big five"—and yet rarely killed

unless in defense of self or property and for

ceremonial reasons.

Like the lion, Maasai warriors roam freely,

make love when they wish, promenade

arrogantly, and attack with a speed swifter

than the mind's reaction.

Of the visitors to camp, Sekerot's and my favorite was

Kardasha, who was not only bright but natural and

enthusiastic in his wish to help us.

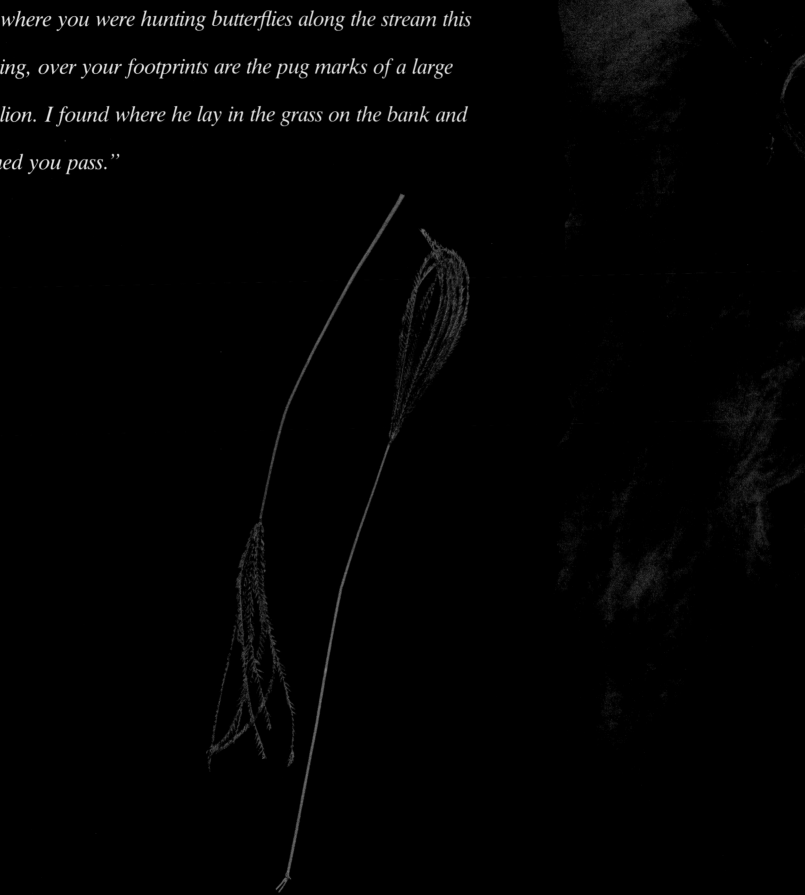

"*Do you know,*" *came Sekerot's voice from inside the tent,* "*that where you were hunting butterflies along the stream this morning, over your footprints are the pug marks of a large male lion. I found where he lay in the grass on the bank and watched you pass.*"

It was when I was taking this portrait that Kardasha

suggested to Sekerot that in the Maasai tradition I call

him, and he me, by a special name. "What do you want

to call Ol ashumpai?" Sekerot asked the boy. "I feel he

is a special friend—'Ol chorelai'—and that is the name I

would give him," answered Kardasha.

Behind Kardasha's strikingly luminous and sometimes

fierce eyes, was a kind, inquisitive, quiet,

straightforward youth.

Since returning to the past was impossible for our Maasai friends, in a small way I hoped to help some of them into their questionable future. Ntiti and Sameri I was able to send to school. Kardasha was too old and traditional for that kind of education. So the only way it seemed I could make his life immediately better was to sponsor his circumcision, which was long overdue and therefore an embarrassment to him and his family.

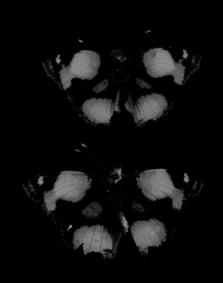

Seldom were black shapes not soaring in the sky above the tent.

Some sailed so high that they barely specked the clouds. Others

passed so near to the ground that their gliding shadows were

seemingly larger than the birds that cast them.

Birds are rarely killed by Maasai except for headdresses used

by recently circumcised boys. Once skinned, this snow-

headed robin chat will be pegged with thorns to a wooden

mannequin. When dry and stuffed with grass it will then be

carefully mummy-wrapped in cloth and stored for a day that,

to many anxious boys, seems will never arrive.

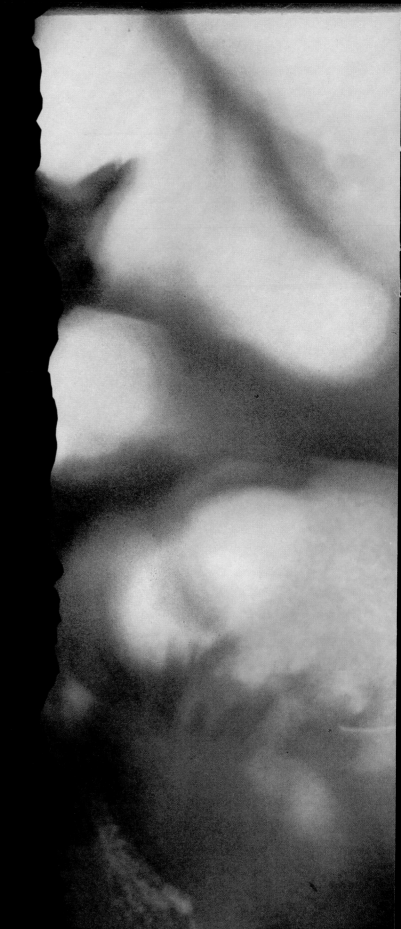

Shortly after four in the morning, several mustard-eyed curs at the

downstream Maasai corral barked with a fury that overlay their

fear, announcing that a leopard had leapt in and then out of the

enclosure with a goat or a sheep in its jaws. Minutes later, from a

tree two hundred yards distant, baboons proclaimed the leopard's

passing, after which he padded by the tent while grating the stillness

At the pinnacle of a Maasai youth's life is the day of his circumcision, the moment his body takes on the physical appearance seen only in men, at which time he proves if he is one or not. This act, which may occur anytime between the early teens and the mid-twenties, can become an all-consuming obsession: wanting to exchange the limited rights of childhood for the respect and freedom of becoming a man.

Now and then we sighted recently circumcised

boys: They appeared alone or in numbers,

shrouded black and haloed with the bodies of half

a hundred stuffed birds fashioned and supported

by sticks into sinister-looking headdresses in a

display of recently acquired manhood.

With the bird boy's growing sense of manly worth blossoms an

arrogance almost without parallel. This period in their lives ends when

their heads are shaved, cleansing the way to the Maasai heaven on

earth—that of the moran, the warrior.

Women in files, at first thin lines, like

brilliant spokes leading to the hub of the

enkang, were not only ochered but wore

their finest beadwork, tinkling head

ornaments, and collar after collar of the most

vivid mixed colors.

129

As tradition defined, instead of bringing his family's cattle in at dusk, Kardasha accompanied them to the corral at noon, after which, on the dung-carpeted floor of the enclosure, he sat amid their lowing. This was the same place where the following day he would be circumcised. Next his head was shaven slick. If at dawn he winced under the knife, it would be said that I had bad judgment for having selected a coward for a son.

In the center of this jubilant, speculative crowd,

Kardasha appeared strikingly alone. Only when

he moved out of the crowd and paused

surrounded by cattle, did I sense he might have felt

some connection with his surroundings.

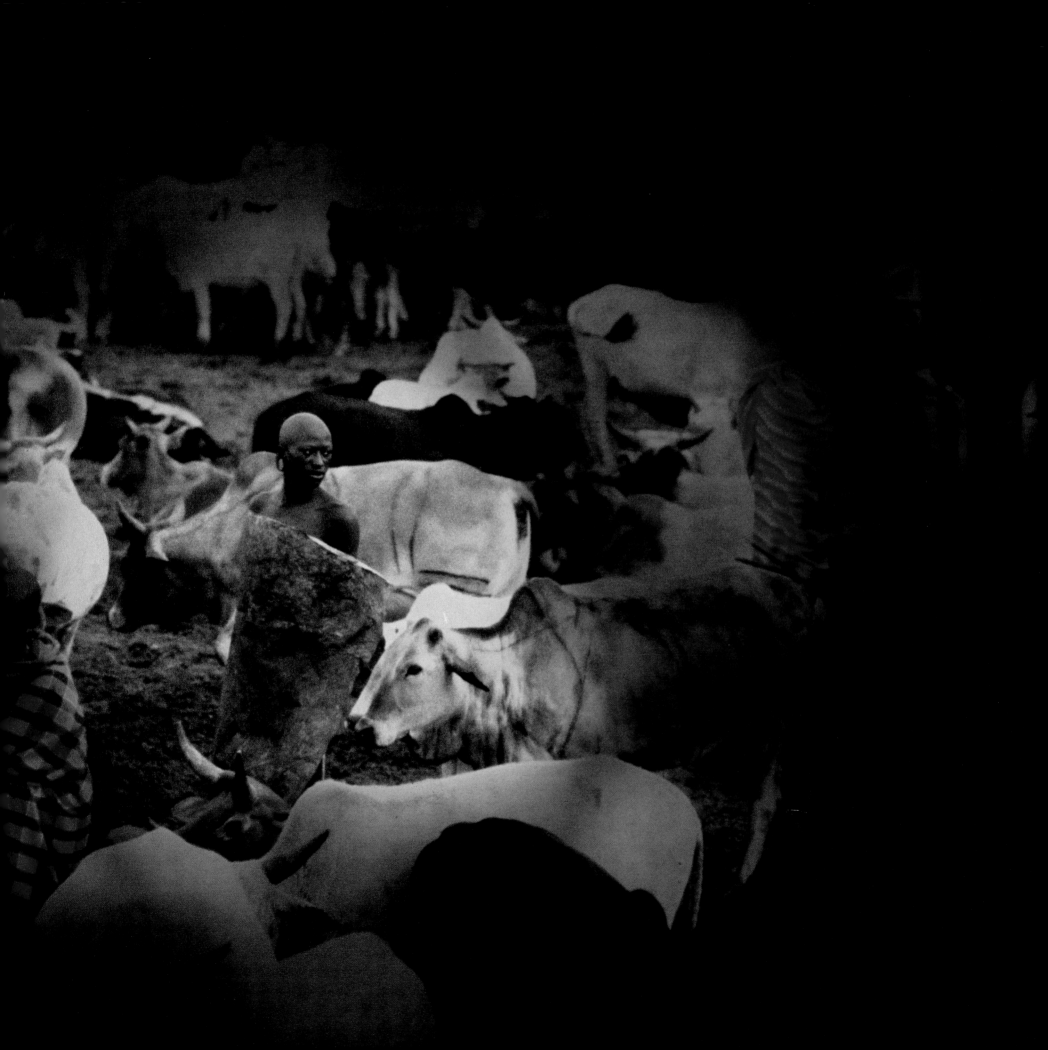

As the Ndorobo circumciser's knife made seemingly

infinite cuts, Kardasha's face communicated absolute

absence from the act. In the holder's arms, his body

remained as flaccid as one imagines was Christ's on the

cross.

At first the girls' indistinguishable voices

came and went with the whims of the breeze.

But, drawing closer, we heard clear

chorused songs which announced the joy of

this day. For some of them, the boy they

celebrated might soon be lover and one day

a husband.

brightness. Suddenly, I experienced a glow that persisted within my being and without. Was Kardasha's celebration cause for this rare state? Not entirely. I think the glow was simply and merely at last feeling a part of Africa, of fitting that piece of myself into the one empty space in the puzzle of my existence.

Kardasha's grandmother and another old woman practically

fell before us, bestowing every blessing possible upon my

person. She now had another son, and a white one at that.

Not to be taken lightly was this proud, honest family's

expression of heartfelt gratitude.

Just before Sameri and me was a stand of gray brush, tall

enough to conceal the elephants that we could hear but not

see. "They are right there. Yes," he whispered as we crept

forward, close enough to hear their stomachs gurgling.

The old man looked into my eyes and spoke, "The

world is a foolish place. The color of skin does not

reveal the taste of the fruit it covers. Your shell is white,

mine is black. But our blood, which is of like color, is

moved by hearts which beat to the same rhythm."

Here, girls before adolescence were famous
among warriors for techniques of lovemaking.
Soon Kardasha would be free to be seduced by
their smiles and to conquer all females around
him, limited only by his stamina.

During these walks or rides in the highlands, warriors seldom crossed our paths. A youth cannot enter into warriorhood alone. The basic rule that a moran must eat in the company of another warrior would in itself make solo entry an impossibility.

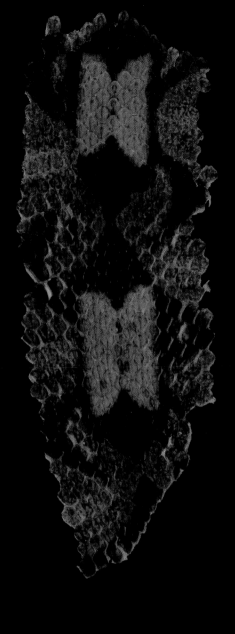

Those moran that we did meet,

however, were unpredictable, arrogant,

accustomed to having their own way

and satisfied with little else—but more

than anything, they were totally

fascinating.

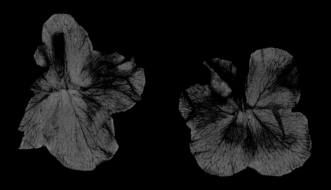

As time approached for me to leave Ololasurai, I

wondered how it would be to live away from this place

where I felt alive as never before. What would mornings

be like without Ntiti's smile and bird-like voice?

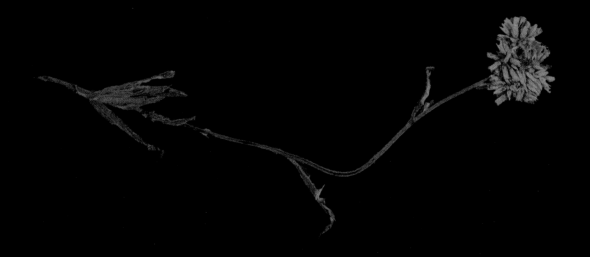

Sometimes I would sit up late at the fire and Moseka

would begin to sing. His voice in the flickering darkness

was as pleasing to the ear as was the cracking campfire

and the night sounds that accompanied it. Sitting around

the dying embers with men whose language I did not

speak or understand was not uncomfortable, for their

presence alone provided comfort and companionship

Usually, as darkness fell and I neared camp, a

figure would appear—either Morkau or Moseka—

whose features would be indistinguishable in the

approaching darkness. They would then walk

behind, hurrying me along like herdsmen urging

forward cattle that had been lost or strayed and, in

the going light, risked not returning at all.

How long would it be, I wondered, before I would return here, if I

returned at all? Living a choice life is frequently given little importance

until it ends, and my days at Ololasurai had so passed until these last

moments of reflection. The sound of a Maasai walking stick tapping

stone brought me from those thoughts. Against the blue of the hillside

a lone figure was racing night to reach his enkang upstream.

By the glow of the lantern that Morkau had left in the tent, I began to write: "For five weeks in the summer of 1989, not another white face—except my own in a cracked mirror—would darken the camp, which was in the hills that rise to the southeast above Maasai Mara. There, I would be gifted with an opportunity few men enjoy. . . .

Prologue Continued
&
Remembering Ololasurai

(continued from page 8)

Months blurred, seventeen of them, before some reality began filtering into that fantasy. As my first African adventure was instigated by Dr. William Wheeler, so was this second safari made possible by him when in California he introduced me to his guest, Sekerot Ole Mpetti. This handsome Maasai youth with flashing eyes and smile not only spoke English, but had as fast and profound a mind and boundless sense of humor as one could chance upon anywhere. Sekerot had been rewarded with a paid vacation to America by two white friends, one of them Wheeler, who had been privileged with his company in Kenya. Provided with a formal education by his late father, a head warden of the Maasai Mara reserve, my new friend was now in the business of doing small, personal safaris. As unlikely as was that encounter was the place the Maasai and I shook hands—on the sands of Solana Beach. By the time the sun had disappeared into the Pacific, Sekerot and I had started planning five weeks together above the Maasai Mara where he had grown up and, in his twenty-seven years, had never seen a white man, except two he had accompanied there. I told him I wanted to set up a tent and not move, except on foot, for thirty-five days. I wanted to know as best I could one small portion of Kenya, its soil, stones, plants, and wildlife. Even five weeks seemed ridiculously little time to do so. Bobbing around like a cork at sea did not seem the way to become acquainted with a place. One small island, a single piece of ground, was what I sought, where I could sit or walk a few steps while watching the immediate world as it passed, instead of having it watch me. I wanted to live with that place, and in so doing learn something about its life, which, for a time, would become my own.

Sekerot seemed to grasp why I wished to completely avoid white people, whether Africans or foreigners. So he promised not only to take me to a pristine paradise called Ololasurai, but to enlist from his village four or five Maasai friends to accompany us. In the ensuing months, as I dreamt again of embracing Kenya, something occurred that would gild the trip in African colonial romance. By some rare fortune, Bill Wheeler, the great adventurer, decided to put into reality his plan for a three-hundred-mile turn-of-the-century horse safari, from Lake Naivasha in Kenya to Lake Natron in Tanzania and back again, accompanied by an entourage of two mares, five donkeys, Sekerot, and several other Maasai. Generously, he offered to loan me the horses once the trip was finished.

However, by the time that summer of 1989 was approaching and Kenya was a brief month away, a storm of changing moods swept away much of the joy that dreams of the trip, a short time before, had stirred in me. The recent death of the person I loved most, together with almost a quarter-century of a self-imposed book-a-year schedule, had left my mind and body depleted. Sitting in the park-like garden of my ranch in Spain, surrounded by outward signs of professional success, I found myself hopelessly without illusion. Preparing for the flight to Kenya, I did so in a workmanlike way, going through the motions, empty of feelings. While packing, I questioned a friend who was helping me: "Should I take these sixty rolls of film? What kind of book can I do in five weeks?" If the duration of the stay was not inhibiting enough, more so were the African favorites that lined the bedroom bookshelves. Most of them I had loved and, again and again, either read their words or marveled at their pictures. The illustrated books on wildlife had been done mainly in the reserves by photographers who had spent months or years with approachable subjects. I would be out of the parks, where the animals were still wildly shy of man, and then there only five weeks. For some of the same reasons, to try a book on Maasai seemed as unlikely. I glanced at *West with the Night* and *Out of Africa,* embarrassed that the thought of attempting a book while in Kenya had at all crossed my mind. Not even in Beryl Markham's words could be found solace: "There are as many Africas as there are books about Africa—and as many books about it as you could read in a leisurely lifetime. Whoever writes a new one can afford a certain complacency in the knowledge that his is a new picture agreeing with no one else's, but likely to be haughtily disagreed with by all of those who believe in some other Africa."

My girlfriend, however, convinced me to take the film, and two cameras instead of one. Sevilla-Madrid-London-Nairobi was the route I followed in a numbed state of limbo, not knowing what to expect upon getting off the last plane, and at the same time expecting nothing. What a mercurial swing from the joyous safari-planning short months before at Solana Beach with Sekerot, whose countenance I could now hardly recall.

Sekerot! Suddenly I saw him among the mostly black crowd of welcomers at Kenyatta Airport. His beaming face, the same one (but unochered) that illuminates page one of this book, instantly ignited feelings inside of me that brought back the Africa that had lain dormant in my soul. I felt a new man, and my Maasai friend appropriately greeted me with a new name, Inkirragat ("my campfire companion"). Maasai intimates never employ given first names, but a pet name, which, when voiced by one, is echoed by the other in response. It was at that moment that this book began.

Remembering Ololasurai

Ololasurai, meaning "place of the snake," was the uninviting name for an isolated valley in the low hills above Maasai Mara. Sekerot took me there with the promise of a campsite, where our tent would have a view of Africa as it had always been. Once the Land-Rover had crashed through roadless bush for miles, become stuck in and, muddied black, spun out of a stream, it came to rest on a rise that overlooks much of Ololasurai. I felt that "Place of the Serpent" was appropriate for the land that spread out before us, which was, indeed, Eden.

From the knoll under a lightning-split fever tree which I chose for our tent, one's eyes were led to the east by a variegated emerald canopy, beneath which passed a brook that serenaded   not more than sixty yards from the tent. This stream flowed—eventually to empty into the Nile—toward a high green hill, Olobiletai, that was part of a range which cradled us. Here, my binoculars were often focused for hours on browsing elephants ambling about in the distance like gray boulders set in motion. When mist or rain gauzed the mountain from view, squeals, trumpeting, and rumbling rolled out across the valley to tell us that the elephants were present.

Directly in front of the tent was a meadow where impala stags battled in copper or silver flashes; depending upon the time of day or night. Ironically, they proclaimed their presence in sawing calls, like that of the leopard, but voiced with more rapidity and punctuated inappropriately with sea-lion roars and blowing. Horn was struck and rattled against horn while the does that waited for them were barely distinguishable from the ocher-rust background but for their ear markings and limpid onyx eyes.

On the far side of the meadow another stream, bordered high with fever trees, umbrella acacias, sandpaper and African ebony trees, flowed to intercept the one which provided water and music for our camp. Farther from the tent and Maasai friends, this was, at first, a mysteriously exotic and inhibiting place, fresh and fragrant after the heat of the meadow and darkened by leaves in as many shades of green and shapes as one could imagine. Vervet monkeys curiously stared from this cool cover, frequently standing upright, heads shifting to and fro as if caught up in a Balinese ballet. They would then swing off through the canopy overhead, which was supported by great towering trunks and gnarled roots of wild figs and other ficuses. Here, often above the sound of water over stone, came the snap of a twig or swish of scales through the grass, lancing my heart into seemingly audible beats of fear. Elephant, Cape buffalo, lion, leopard, mamba, cobra, adder, and viper lived where we did. However, as time passed, this terror was replaced mostly by cautious apprehension. Here, bushbacks, rich syrupy flashes in shafts of sunlight, bounded off, leaving dark wakes in the tall grass, next to which washed sand was embossed with the pug marks of big cats, as well as those of genets and servals.

Beyond the stream, the land rose rocky, with patchy clearings, until a hundred yards up wedges of forest arrowed to a long wavy ridge plumed with carissa shrubs. Now and then this undulated crest was patrolled by a solitary giraffe, which cut a striking silhouette against the lonely sky.

To the left of the tent was a long valley that ended in a wall of mountain, eroded and pitted with caves which once had been home to prehistoric dwellers. These refuges in stone were now inhabited by baboons and by a band of Ndorobo hunters, who, the morning of my arrival, had made a kill. A bull giraffe had risen to watch the dawn, not knowing it would be his last.

Behind the tent was a low ridge, not long ago burned off by fire set by the pastoral, semi-nomadic Maasai to stimulate new grazing for their sheep, goats, and cattle. Midday often blew hot breath to cast a saffron pall over this hill where zebra stomped the charred ground, pluming their hooves in eruptions of ash while calling in voices more like those of yapping lapdogs than of the earth's most exotic equines. From this same mountain of cinder twisted the gnarled trunks of wild olive trees, and beneath one of these lived a cobra the diameter of my bicep and seemingly as long as my nightmares about it.

Upstream from the tent, the water changed color to that of flowing lava, reflecting the red canopy of wait-a-bit thorn trees, whose branches at dusk were shaken by baboons that peered menacingly. Farther along this slight waterway was a spacious meadow shaded by umbrella acacias, a glorious scene which was more romantic than the painted backdrop of any natural history museum's African waterhole exhibit.

Rocky cliffs soared high above the acacia tops, haunting pinnacles and protrusions of stone, where klipspringers hopped and played. Occasionally on these boulders, in the early morning sun, honey-coated lions were seen, their draped forms tired and bulging from the hunt. The top of this mountain, which was at its best when silhouetted against boiling cumulus, was covered in high grass and brush, through which we moved cautiously in search of Cape buffalo and their nests of smashed vegetation. It was here that, droopy-eyed, they chewed cuds during the hot daylight hours.

The plain below Ololasurai was a constant parade of stomping hooves, a pageant of horn, stripes, and spots, exotically marked and tinted, yet subtle to the eye. There were great phalanxes and endless files of migrating wildebeest, whose numbers were such that they could no more easily be counted than grains of sand on the shore. Croaking in deep bullfrog voices, they plodded determinedly ahead, accompanied by handsome escorts of zebra and Thomson's and Grant's gazelle. Ostrich, kori bustards, ground hornbills, and secretary birds often kept pace with this flood of fur that swept across the flat land, adding to its splendor with their feathered finery. This spectacle was viewed by the plains residents, as evocative in their appearance as were the migrants who passed before them. Giraffe peered down through lacy acacia leaves. From the top of anthill craters, slate-flanked rouged topis stared, and warthogs trotted off in short jarring steps, cutting the breeze with their tails straight-up.

Above and around the tent the sky was not only prismed with wings, but pierced, warbled, hooted, boomed, and trilled with duets, choruses, and fugues of bird voices, except sometimes at midday, when the air was still, but for the wings of solitary cicada. Directly behind the tent was a black-scarred, long-deceased acacia, well over one hundred feet tall, which reached straight up to divide into a number of boughs, the center branch being the tallest. The extremity of this charred limb ended in twists of black that, fortunately for us, was the most attractive perch for birds within a mile of the tent.

Early morning brought a matrimony of hadada ibises to this inviting roost, announcing their arrival with resounding "haar-har, harrras," which, except for that of the lion, is the most African of sounds to many ears. Maasai call these raucous birds "the donkeys of the highlands." Once on the branch, the ibises peered down at us with clear-irised eyes, while turning red curved beaks from side to side. The male of this pair, larger and darker than his mate, glittered purple, green, and black, a mosaic of irides-

cent flashes against the freshness of the morning blue.

After the last ibis cries had echoed down the valley, a pair of lilac-breasted rollers startled the sky with their cries and brilliant plumage before arrowing upward in flight, then acrobatically zooming and twisting at great speed to the acacia perch. This tree was also the bedtime roost to a duo of white-backed vultures, who, silhouetted against the darkening sky, seemed unusually sinister.

The vegetation along the stream provided cover for an assortment of avian life richer than that contained in most birdwatchers' guides: tropical boubous, D'Arnaud's and red and yellow barbets, blue-naped and speckled mousebirds, cardinal woodpeckers, giant and malachite kingfishers, hammerkops, grey flycatchers, paradise flycatchers, Ross's and Schalow's turacos, yellow-vented bulbuls, northern brownbuls, hill babblers, stonechats, olive thrushes, snowy-headed robin chats, yellow white-eyes, black-headed orioles, white-bellied go-away-birds, African hoopoes, brown parrots, little bee-eaters, red-billed hornbills, African scops owls, Verreaux's eagle owls, red-eyed doves, laughing doves, and speckled pigeons.

The shrubs directly around the tent's rainfly were constantly ornamented by a communion of red, green, blue, crimson, gray, white, orange, lavender, gold, yellow, and black flashes, as if decorated for some never-ending holiday celebrating life. Above this collage of brilliant plumage came voices from my long-ago boyhood and the aviary I kept, with my father's help, in Glendale, California: firefinches, green-backed twinspots, bronze mannikins, silverbills, red-cheeked cordon-bleus, pin-tailed whydahs, bishops and black-headed weavers, purple grenadiers, black-headed and common waxbills, and golden-breasted waxbills.

Taller twigs and branches were used by Ruppell's

long-tailed starlings, superb starlings, violet-backed starlings, fiscal shrikes, and grey-headed bush shrikes. From the hills around the tent, flocks of helmeted guineafowl, crested francolins, and yellow-necked spurfowl cackled and chattered.

Black shapes were forever soaring in the sky above the rainfly's greenness. Some sailed so high that they barely specked the blue or white. Others passed so near to the ground that their gliding shadows were seemingly larger than the birds that cast them: bateleurs, marabou storks, white-backed vultures, tawny eagles, hooded vultures, martial eagles, and augur buzzards. Before rain fell, Nyanza swifts swarmed far above the tent, then cascaded toward us, their crescent wings cutting the air in audible ruffles. The underside of the rainfly provided a well-protected surface, to which wire-tailed swallows attached their nests of mud.

The insect life around us was as extensive and evocative as was the variety of birds. However, being almost six thousand feet above sea level made the netting of our tent unnecessary, for I never saw a mosquito at Ololasurai. Tsetse flies infrequently visited camp, though safari ants unexpectedly ribboned the ground in massive pulsations of red and black. Once I awoke to the horses' stomping hooves and their cries in the night. The ants had marched into the confines of the corral to swarm over panicked Katie and Narok, the mares that Bill Wheeler had lent us. Moseka, our Maasai groom, haltered the horses and led them into the open, but not before he and they had been bitten from head to foot.

Until cattle came, there were few small flies around Ololasurai, and then, being nonbiting, they were of little bother if one decided to ignore their fine legs tickling the edges of eyes and ears. In fact, I was grateful for their presence and thought of them as allies. A lioness lying in dry grass the color of her hide would have seemed not there at all until an ear twitched to shoo away the flies that crawled and hummed around it.

By midmorning, butterflies drifted above the meadow on their way to the cool moisture and seductive blossoms of the stream. The awkward net I had fashioned from ripped mosquito netting, a wire coat hanger, and a piece of branch was of little use, except for catching smaller varieties that flew low to the ground and lit often. There was one large yellow, unattainable prize that resembled a pair of autumn leaves stitched together, but these soared too high, out of reach of the net. Often I dashed along the stream, caught up in the chase. However, no state of excitement prevented me from also searching the ground for the black of a mamba or for a cobra's coils.

Several former Maasai warriors who were hired to help tend our camp at first found amusement in my mostly ineffective attempts to catch butterflies with the makeshift net. As they watched, I felt like some eccentric, pale-faced Victorian sissy who went after his prey with a bit of lace instead of with a spear of steel. However, as time passed and with the arrival of a professional net, it was then difficult to keep this new toy out of the hands of men who before were accustomed to hunting only Cape buffalo, lion, and leopard. There was joy in watching the Maasai rushing across the clearing, one with the net while the others, arms and spears waving, tried to "herd" some high-flying beauty and keep it from reaching the surrounding patches of forest. No less exuberance or determination would have shown in their expressions had they been attempting to turn back the entire Serengeti wildebeest migration.

Heavy rains changed the hills from ebony to emerald to jade, which was as attractive to our eyes as it was to the 167 increasing numbers of zebra and impala that began descending on Ololasurai. Good grazing also summoned animals that were not wild. Evening brought currents of black, white, chocolate, chestnut, liver, tan, and gray as cattle flowed down and along twists of waving August-dried stalks and seedheads that cut ocher through the forest green. Herd boys sang and whistled, bells sounded in a chorus of tone, while turacos announced the coming of these processions in voices seemingly too loud for the size of their emerald bodies.

As we watched evening fall on the tent and the vibrant tones of day gray to announce approaching darkness, it was like waiting for lights in a cinema to dim so that the spectacle of night could commence. The blackness, however, was not devoid of light as stars sparkled above and fireflies glimmered in patches of vegetation around us. The eyes of genet cats, servals, and jackals—ruby, emerald, and topaz chips—flashed back to the torch's glare as I walked to our recently set-up outhouse, which appeared close to the tent during daylight; night, however, elongated its distance enough to cause some uneasiness. The warped plastic toilet seat fit its metal frame very loosely, which after dark always caused me to flash the torch into the hole to see if a mamba or cobra had taken refuge there.

Then, as I would peer out into nothingness, trousers around my ankles, I would think of a small boy trembling with fear, crouched on a similar but wooden seat at our uncle's remote ranch near Hemet, California. My imagination would project cougars from the film *My Friend Flicka* into the trees above the outhouse. After pulling up my pants, I would step into the darkness, a flickering kerosene lamp in the seemingly distant cabin as a beacon, sure with each step I would feel the mountain lion's claws rip through the red-flannel shirt on my back.

Now I sat in the blackness of Ololasurai as a hyena hoooooooped, a sound my ears looked forward to as a heralder of the drama that all around us had started to unfold. Here, each hyena had its own voice, easily distinguishable to others of its clan, and even to me. Jackals keened. Lions put thunder into the cloudless night, and a leopard sawed the darkness with his rough call. Baboons barked alarm downstream and then quarreled, terrorizing the blackness with screams that seemed could only end in death. Rainy evenings cast fairy-tale wonder in the fever boughs above the tent, moisture beading and shimmering from the branches in millions of starry droplets, while the light from our torches was reflected in the fiery opal eyes of a half dozen bushbabies. While clutching the lime bark with bony, miniature hands, they stared down at us like demons from a Flemish painting.

From ten o'clock to when each morning I awoke at four, there were few sounds to stir our sleep. But at that hour began the final act that would end with first light of dawn. Anticipation of what was to come brought me, without fail, to consciousness every night I spent in the tent. However, there were times when, from sunset to break of day, hardly a sound was heard. Once, though, on my cot in the darkness, it seemed that even the conversation of safari ants, though spoken in whispers, could not escape my hearing, which had been accentuated by rhubarb-red miraa, stems which are pulled through the teeth, stripped and chewed to stimulate the senses.

Shortly after four, several mustard-eyed curs at the downstream Maasai settlement, or *enkang*, barked with a fury that overlay their fear, announcing that a leopard had leapt in and then out of the enclosure with a goat or sheep in its jaws. (An enkang is a permanent corral of thorn, in-

corporating family huts in its perimeter.) Lions sounded promptly, to reveal they had confiscated and were disputing the leopard's catch. In minutes, baboons barked from a tree two hundred yards downstream, to proclaim the leopard's passing, after which he padded by the tent grating the stillness with his throaty call. Ten minutes later a scruffy caramel-colored mutt from the upstream enkang yapped to indicate that the leopard was either stalking outside the thorn enclosure or had already made his kill, which he would afterward deposit in the fork of an acacia tree that, near the spires of rock, served as his larder.

Following this, there was stillness until about five-thirty, when lions lamented the first trace of light and hyenas whooped, retreating into a wedge of dusky mountain forest behind the tent.

Then there was quiet until faint clouds overhead were fringed coral to summon a single bird song, which, in minutes, was joined by another and another, each distinct from the rest, like instruments of an orchestra warming up for concert. Of the daylong musical program that continued, a favorite number was voiced by a pair of dueting tropical boubous calling back and forth to one another with such precision that it seemed impossible the voice belonged to two birds instead of one. The song they provided was clear and far-carrying, like that of an unoiled but deep-toned pump.

How could anyone, Hemingway and Blixen included, be disappointed with the view from the tent with which Sekerot had provided me? To this setting, the mares Katie and Narok arrived like half-expected lottery prizes. Bill Wheeler had purchased the gaunt Thoroughbreds near Lake Naivasha. From there he and Sekerot had ridden them down the Rift Valley and back across into the Loita Hills, where, had it not been for the veterinary supplies they carried, both animals, relentlessly bitten by tsetse flies, would have perished. Months later, when they trotted into our camp, their bodies were still pebbled with welts.

The company of animals, not people, was what we desired around camp, so the mares were welcome companions. Grazing in tall grass before the tent or on the other side of the stream, they were watched over, whispered and sung to by Moseka, a quietly handsome Tanzanian Maasai. In his care they seemed as unaware of danger from lions and leopards, whose pug marks trespassed their hoofprints, as if they had been pastured in some Sussex meadow. Elephants, however, did make the mares anxious. When an adolescent bull crashed and pulled branches, browsing across the stream from the corral, they fidgeted and snorted even under the quiet reassurance from Moseka, for whom they seemed to feel special trust and affection. Horse odors, neighs, and nickers added another perspective to the camp, and I found fraternity and peace in their presence, as I have in the company of equines everywhere.

At Ololasurai, the discomforts for which Africa has a reputation were almost nonexistent. Snakes rarely crossed the shadow of the tent. Mosquitos, as I have said, were a nonoccurrence, and though the sun sometimes was relentlessly intense before rain, days at camp were never uncomfortably warm. Typical dress was long-sleeved cotton shirts and trousers. Nights were cool enough for a chamois shirt and down jacket.

When we had initiated our search for a campsite, I had asked Sekerot if we might find a place that was little visited, even by native people. That first Kenyan memory of aggressive, tourist-spoiled Maasai had left me with little wish to deal with them on this trip. In our first days at Ololasurai, the fact that much of the grazing land around camp had been intentionally burned off and that no rain had come to sprout rich new growth delighted me, for it meant that, except for a passing relative of Sekerot's coming or going to his enkang four miles away, we would be left undisturbed. As time passed in this idyllic place, I blamed my girlfriend for convincing me to lug around dozens of rolls of film and two cameras, for, after a week, the only pictures I had taken were with my eyes, to be recorded on the fading film of my memory.

While we were continually in the presence of wildlife here, out of the reserve, not even the camera bag's longest telephoto lens would bring anything close enough for an acceptable image. My imagination scanned every possible nature-book idea. But it seemed that all things evocative had been done, and though there were Maasai in the vicinity, I was convinced that the Beckwith and Saitoti's *Maasai* had sealed the possibility of anyone else doing a book on those handsome people. Besides, I no longer enjoyed pointing a camera at persons, like Maasai, who did not wish to be photographed.

Finally, as if scheduled, the rains did come every afternoon between three and five, cumulus gathering above the mountains to the east, while beyond the camp the sky darkened. In minutes, the black cotton soil would be drenched and water would be flooding around the earth platform upon which the tent had been wisely set. While lightning illuminated the unseen world outside, accompanied by exuberant rolls of thunder, I stretched out, dry and warm, on my cot and transcribed notes, paged through bird guides, reread Myles Turner's *My Serengeti Years*, and started *Serengeti Home*, which his widow, Kay, had recently given me in Nairobi. These books and papers were not kept in order, but scattered on the floor around a too-tall night table. For weeks during my first safari I had twisted nightly in a sleeping bag on the stony ground. I had been unable to bathe until I did not care if I stank or not. I had done my laundry by swishing clothes in muddy water that often left them more stained than before. I had been too exhausted at day's end to have to cook a grubby meal, and even worse, afterward, in the darkness, I had to scrub dishes that were never without a film of grease. Now I promised myself that at Ololasurai we would live in modest comfort. Also, for half a lifetime studying bulls and horses I had too often roughed it in the wild from dawn to dawn and was ready for a change.

So, now we had a tent large enough for two cots, a table, our clothes, cameras, and books. A tubular metal structure supported a canvas rainfly overhead. We had a three-burner stove, tables, camp chairs, a portable wash basin, a canvas-bag shower that was hung over smooth, flat stream stones, curtained by a circular screen of cut saplings and leaves, and nightly filled with gallons of hot water. We had a toilet seat attached to a metal frame, beneath which had been dug a ten-foot hole and kept private by another screen fashioned from the surrounding foliage. A one-man tent stored food, while two larger domed ones housed Sicona, Moseka, Lepish, Morkau, and Masiene, the Maasai who cooked our food and served it, built fires, washed clothes and dishes, cared for the horses, and kept the campsite tidy. Until Sekerot came into their lives as an employer, most of these men gave no thought to tossing trash on the ground. Maasai association with plastic, I guessed, had been too brief for them to realize that this material, unlike a banana peel or shred of paper, resisted deterioration by the tropical elements. However, perhaps they did know and simply did not care. At first, I wondered whether I chose to believe Maasai were something they were not, like falling in love with someone for the way they appear, not the way they are, looking beyond a stare to see something where there is nothing.

Much to everyone's amusement, I forever found new projects, the biggest of which was building a 150-yard network of large flat stones which kept our feet dry while going from tents to the campfire, to the kitchen, shower, and toilet, and to my office, a circular platform of raised earth surfaced with loose-fitting slabs of rock joined together like puzzle pieces. This "office," as it was called, where a chair and table with a typewriter were set, commanded a view of the stream where the endless display of birds listed earlier continually distracted me from the typewriter keys. Birds, however, were not the only diversion. Maasai boys sometimes sat or stood around the table giggling, as I pounded out in caps, ink on paper, names which were theirs, but which most of them could neither read nor relate to their identity. However, Turere, who was enrolled in school, corrected me when a finger missed a key and "called" was written "calld." "You have forgotten the 'e,'" he proudly said, smudging both the paper with the tip of a dirty finger, as well as my reputation as an author of books. After all, if one had to be corrected by a fourth-level Maasai from the most primitive of schools, what sort of writer might one be? Naturally, after several such mistakes, partly mine, partly those of the rented typewriter, my literary ability was placed in doubt.

Apart from spelling, the boys taught things of more

meaning to my new life: that pulling grass is a sign of forgiveness, for example, and that one never points at the sun, moon, stars, and sky with his index finger, but with the thumb protruding between the index and middle fingers. However, in spite of the birds, boys, and misspelled words, if one could not write a decent sentence in this "office," then chances were it would never happen. Ololasurai was the most perfect place for working I had ever known. Here, there were no distractions except those I sought. No telephone. No car to deal with or repair. No dog, though I dearly loved my Basenji in Spain, to be fed or taken to the vet. No broken water pump to cause days of grief. No electricity to fail. No unwanted conversation from the people around me who were so soft-spoken they hardly were there at all; and when I did hear their words, which I could not understand, it was like listening to the sweet voices of birds that sang from the bushes along the stream.

There was also no caretaker demanding higher wages. No unwanted guests arriving unannounced on the doorstep. No newspapers to bring tragedy to the breakfast table. No tie and suit in which to feel uncomfortable. No traffic fumes or congestion. At Ololasurai there would always be water as long as a never-dry stream carried it. There would always be warmth and light as long as we had matches to start the fire; and even without them, the Maasai could manage. There would always be companionship as long as animals and birds who had forever lived here did not vanish. There would be no breakdown in transportation unless one broke a leg or hip. The list could continue, evidence that what is wrong for one man is right for another.

As time passed, some faces among the workers at camp were replaced by others. One left for being drunk, another because of a hot temper, and one because he learned too slowly. But others arrived at the tent searching for employment and new experience. Some had to be dismissed. Others stayed on and were far better than the men they replaced. Laundering clothes, cooking, washing dishes, and sewing were acts that Maasai machismo normally excluded from the lives of the men who came to work for us. But most of our friends mastered these chores with accomplishment, acceptance, and without complaint. The camp was frequently graced by the presence of Miton, a tall Loita Maasai of kingly countenance and Sekerot's best friend. Infrequently, when a Land-Rover was needed, Miton was at camp to provide us with transportation.

On most afternoons weather changes brought delightful combinations of golden light and platinum showers. With these storms, one never knew what to expect, for they could envelop Ololasurai as rapidly as they would afterward disappear.

One punished our camp with excessive fury. Sekerot and I had been joking in the tent when the first patter sounded off the rainfly. In an instant, the late afternoon sky darkened, as if night had rescheduled its arrival. Thunder boomed and lightning flashed the rainfly a neon green. Wind filled the inside of our refuge, lashing and whipping it until a great wave of air ripped the 160-pound pipe structure, along with six square meters of canvas, from the ground, and carried the rainfly off, who could determine where.

With the protective rainfly gone, there seemed not the slightest chance that the naked tent could withstand surging blast after blast of air and water. As one tent stake and pole after another were torn from the ground, the canvas began to collapse. Sekerot and I stood with our arms spread upward, hopeful of providing the cloth with some support, sure that the next bolt of electricity would strike our fingers and pass through our bodies into the earth.

For an hour, when not smiling anxiously at each other, we shouted for help to the smaller tents, not knowing if they were still standing or not. But our pleas went unattended. Unable to contain himself any longer, Sekerot rushed out into the fury to search for the rainfly, which, hopefully, had not already been ripped beyond repair. Suddenly, the rain stopped and the wind fell. The storm had passed. Currents of black water eddied round the tent as Sekerot and the others returned carrying the bent pipes and slashed green canvas of the rainfly. I could hardly keep a long face with the Maasai joking and laughing as the fires were being lit and Sekerot was asking Sicona to peel potatoes for the evening meal.

The following morning, the sun sparkled on rich blades of grass, now inches long, that shot up through the black hardening soil, and in the distance, above the cries of a trio of hadada ibis, came the delicate tinkling of sheep and goat bells and the monotonous, but pleasing, bird-like whistles of the uncircumcised boys who attended them. Green had returned to the hills of Africa. Rain not only brought freshness to the surrounding ground cover, but to the flat acacia tops, which, until recently, had been drably stubbled black, but now were turning as emerald as the grass beneath them.

Fire, combined with water, had provided good grazing for Ololasurai and the people of Maa were moving toward the camp. In the days and weeks that followed, few passed by without visiting the tent. Some stayed on and raised temporary corrals and shelter in the valley.

Though bronzed-chocolate was not the color of my skin, African idioms were unintelligible to my ears, and I had never speared a lion, yet an ever-so-slight affinity was established between me and the people who did come to our camp—when Sekerot told them three things. I am mystically moved by cattle. I am circumcised. And several years past, in the depths of a Loita forest, I had, unarmed, leapt from a tree to face a raging Cape buffalo which was seconds from goring and bashing a friend from existence.

The experience with the buffalo, though, was actually the only real bond between the Maasai and me. Circumcision had scarred my unaware body shortly following birth and did not involve the artistic surgery, the stoic test of bravery and concentration which all Maasai youths face upon having their foreskins sliced, cutting the way into manhood.

While I love and raise cattle, the animals I breed in Spain are not docile pets, as are the Maasais' bulls and cows, which provide their owners with sustenance in the form of milk, dung for building houses, status in numbers, and companionship, animals which, when young, sleep in the comfortable confines of their master's homes. My beasts are *toros bravos*, which have no contact with man except for the brand at the age of one or until years later when they die by the sword in some *plaza de toros*. However, like the Maasai, everything about cattle I find appealing: how they look, how they sound, and how they smell. But while the people of Maa adore their animals for placidity, mine are bred to be admired for their ferocity.

In Spain I had left my bulls and cows pasturing in an ocher-colored landscape similar to that of Ololasurai, but enclosed by century-old stone walls that not only restricted their movement but the human eye that sought freedom in the panorama.

At Ololasurai two sizable corrals of thorn branches were built for the nightime use of cattle and their caretakers a quarter of a mile downstream, and as the grass grew in height and abundance, more spacious structures were erected for sheep and goats in the valley above us. The Maasai who began stopping by the tent and campfire were as unlike those I had tried to avoid around the park gates—except in exotic, handsome outward appearance—as were nightingales from crows. The people who came to our tent seldom requested anything except a "hello" or *"jambo"* to their *"supa."* Their hard, lean bodies were a foil to the softness, both in speech and manner, which, along with the traditions that dictated their lives, made them enormously distinct from any men, women, and children who previously had crossed my experience. When it came time for a siesta in late afternoon, I always hoped that some of these visitors would be found sitting, gossiping quietly behind the tent, for when one made a statement, the other responded like the partner of a pair of tropical boubous, with an uuumm-mmmmmm, with an oooohhhhhhh, with an eeehhhhhhh, which, in minutes, lulled me to sleep. Equally intriguing were their subtle finger and hand gestures, used to emphasize a spoken word, which were as distinct from the hysterical hand-waving of the Mediterranean people among whom I usually live as is the body language of a Thai dancer from that of a fishwife flapping out laundry.

I experienced a great affinity with my new friends and felt more comfortable when addressed as "Inkirragat" than when called "Robert." How stiff Western life had made me I realized when Sekerot asked, "Moseka and Morkau want to know why you and most white men walk as rigidly as bulls?" From then on I tried to move more like a

Maasai, like grass with the breeze, to form a natural part of the landscape, not jar it with my American-learned rigidness.

Soon I became acquainted with some of the passersby, those like Ntiti, Turere, Kardasha, Rereu, Pashirei, Kirringae, and Penba, who seemed to enjoy our company. For hours I would sit on a log or stretch out on the grass totally happy in their company, Sekerot's twelve-year-old brother, Sameri, the tongue and ears between me and them. At first, when I lay on the ground, face up, my new acquaintances, with concern, told me to take a bit of grass and put it on my stomach so that, I would not appear dead when seen from the sky. Frequently, as they bade goodbye, they said to Sameri, "Tell him 'thank you' for respecting us and our conversation." These words, heard again and again, were enough to rouse feelings from a stone. What kind of white men, or ideas of them, had they experienced? I wondered. "Ol ashumpai" was what they called me, which is a word for white men (used originally for Arabs) that bears no judgment, unlike the word *ol kaporri*, which has a derogatory connotation. *Ol musungui* was only occasionally used to distinguish me, and this simply means "the European or white man."

Of the boys who visited us, Kardasha and Ntiti seemed not only curious about our horses and camping equipment but especially about me—a white man. While other Maasai youths paused briefly each day for conversation and perhaps a cup of tea, Kardasha, who must have been in his late teens, and Ntiti, who was then about twelve years of age, frequently tagged after me or sat in front of the tent while I was having a siesta. At first smiles were our only communication, apart from a "supa" or "hello" in Maasai. But as time passed, Sekerot or Sameri translated my questions about them and theirs about me.

Occasionally I felt somewhat guilty, knowing that Kardasha and Ntiti should be tending goats or cattle instead of accompanying Sameri and me on short excursions, as fascinated with peering through my binoculars as I was with their comments about the creatures upon which we spied. Behind Kardasha's strikingly luminous and sometimes fierce eyes was a kind, inquisitive, quiet, straightforward boy who with Ntiti soon became my favorite among the Maasai who passed by our camp.

Smiles and laughter were often dimmed when someone arrived to tell us that barking heard the night before was all that remained after a predator had carried off a sheep, goat, cow, or even the dog who had guarded them, animals that had been beckoned by name and had been warm and soft to their master's touch. It took far less effort for a lion or leopard to leap a thorn fence, where night after night they were assured of finding a meal, than for them to cast about the hillsides in quest of prey which had the whole of Ololasurai into which to escape. Frequently, not even the jumping of a barrier was necessary. A lion had only to circle the corral of thorn, spreading his scent, accompanied by the gleam of an eye or the seemingly unnoticeable flick of a tail, to seed panic in the herd. Unable to tolerate the pungent presence outside the enclosure, the cattle would bolt, stampeding, to crash from the protection of the flame-lit corral and into the darkness, and the jaws that were concealed by it.

More often than one would like to think, these nightly raids claimed so many victims—one man lost forty-two of his forty-three sheep—that little choice was offered but to abandon the recently constructed thorn corral and move from the predator's territory to a distant place, where the task of erecting a new enclosure awaited. Watching the abandonment of a corral was painful to me. However,

the Maasai refused to be victims, accepting such an occurrence as a tribute to the nature of which they were also a part. Leopards and lions needed to eat. They had always killed livestock and forever would do so. My friends, without rancor, also accepted taking the life of a predator. Some mornings I visited scenes of the previous night's seemingly morbid happenings. A fence too low. A sleeping dog. A spear that missed its mark. A drag mark here. Grass flecked with dried blood. A tree full of vultures a quarter of a mile away. The story of the night could be read on the surrounding ground as easily as the pages of this book.

The Maasai that I had previously seen away from the tourist routes had been distant, exotic figures, like wild animals spontaneously captured by a camera in documentary images. The Maasai who came to us were people with basic human emotions and responses, like us, but dressed in togas or *shukas*, ornamented with beads and ochers, armed with spears, short swords, and clubs, and framed within what seemed the most attractive of landscapes. What governed their expressions, however, was an iron code of tradition, which not only makes them singular among the earth's beings, but which has allowed them to prevail in a corrupting, hostile, almost overpoweringly seductive white man's consumer, Christian world.

Thinking these thoughts in the darkness of the tent, my mind projected the Spanish faces that I had tried to represent in *Iberia*, a book done with James Michener, and in *The Sevilla of Carmen*. In those portraits I had asked bullfighters, counts, and Gypsy families to look directly into the camera at a time before such portraiture was fashionable, when most cameramen told their subjects to refrain from making eye contact with the lens. It was obvious that the persons photographed were aware of having their pictures taken, and to have them look away in pretended unawareness of the happening seemed artificial. More important to me was the adage that eyes are windows of the soul. Thus, in those Spanish books a reader in Kansas or Hong Kong could make eye contact with a Cordoban matador or a duchess from Madrid. However, it had taken years of living in Spain to gain entry to the faces behind the iron grillwork.

The remainder of that night sleep eluded me. At four-thirty in the morning, I tossed and turned, with no sound to distract my thoughts but the seemingly ceaseless blowing of impala, and it was then that I awoke Sekerot. My great apprehension, I told him, was the awareness that most Maasai resisted, for one reason or another, being photographed, which was, perhaps, why the book of posed intimate portraits that I envisioned had never been attempted. Maybe that was the reason that the majority of photographs of Maasai, other than unimaginative picture postcards, had been taken during traditional ceremonies. There people had been snapped unaware of the camera, like beasts at a waterhole, and seemed ready to attack or bolt at the click of a shutter or reflection of light in a lens.

"A book like that has never been done," spoke Sekerot, his eyes lit by moonlight that filtered through the tent's netted windows. "But it should be done as a record of us as human beings. I also wish to help you, Inkirragat." There was a pause. No sound came from the African night until he added, "We will do it." And so, this book came into being. As Maasai visited the tent, Sekerot convinced them to pose for me. Because his village was nearby, many of these people were childhood friends or relatives. The strangers who passed our way were won over when they learned that Sekerot was the son of Mpetti, the nearby park's former head warden. Apart from being so favored as a "photographer's agent," my friend also had such a rapid mind and winning way that no one who was asked refused to sit or stand before my camera. The rainfly and our camp became a studio. The sky provided lighting; bright yellow grass or the green canvas, reflectors; branches and leaves, filters; the forest and hills, backdrops. In this studio I spent some of the most happily creative days of my life. Maasai beadwork, in other photographs, I felt, distracted from the faces of the people who wore it. In those images, men and women almost seemed present only to showcase the gaudy jewelry with which they were adorned. For this reason, I decided to throw the beadwork out of focus, using wide apertures and fast shutter speeds. If this were successful, the brightly colored unusual earrings, head adornments, necklaces, and bracelets, would enhance my subjects, not overpower them.

Of our "models," Sekerot's and my favorite was Kardasha, who was not only photogenic but bright, natural, and enthusiastic in his wish to help us. Of all the youths who visited the camp, he seemed to most nearly represent the prototype of the Maasai pre-warrior, the boy on the edge of manhood. It was during one of our photographic sessions that he suggested to Sekerot that in the Maasai tradition I call him, and he me, by a special name. "What do you want to call Ol ashumpai?" Sekerot asked the boy.

"I feel he is a special friend—'ol chorelai'—and that is the name I would call him," answered Kardasha. So around camp I was now addressed in four ways. Sekerot called me "Inkirragat." Miton used my given name, "Robert." Most of the Maasai referred to me as "Ol ashumpai." And now I had a new friend who would call me "Ol chorelai." The word *ol chore* means friend and has as many nuances as one cares to give it or feels with its use,

ranging from addressing strangers with "Hey, my friend," to employment with one's companions. Ol chorelai means "my special friend" and is reserved for use by intimates. In Maasailand, one might have as many names as one had acquaintances, friends, and relatives.

As the days passed, even the intensity of those photographic sessions could not distract from my first African passion, Cape buffalo. Overlooked, degraded, and dismissed by tourists as dull and cow-like, Cape buffalo have stirred special feelings in certain men, among them Hemingway, Michener, van der Post, and former Serengeti warden Myles Turner. It was the latter who wrote: "Even in those days it was not the lion or the leopard that gripped my imagination, nor the forest rhino or even the ghostly grey elephants with their gleaming ivory and sail-like ears. It was the African Cape buffalo, the most dangerous of all the 'big five' African game animals, a black truculent creature with a reputation second to none for creating general mayhem.

"Why I find buffalo so fascinating, I cannot say. Maybe it is all wrapped up in that solid 2,000 pound frame, those great, curving horns and extraordinary pale blue eyes. Or maybe it is the nature of the beast, which is of stubborn, unflinching courage and unmitigated revenge should he ever gain the advantage."

To me also, the buffalo embodies Africa. Its corpulence, boss and swing of horn, its reputation for unprovoked, relentless attack, cause one to sense death as a companion, a distillation for me of what I feel in the presence of Africa. With the possibility of extinction men feel more alive, not only because of rushes of adrenaline, but because eyes see more, noses smell scents of which they were never before aware, ears hear sounds that previously seemed not to exist, even touch becomes terribly acute, be it a only cheek passed over by the slightest change of breeze.

This fascination with Cape buffalo, like other things important to my life, surely began with the books of Ernest Hemingway. As a teenager, on the sands of Laguna Beach, I first read *Death in the Afternoon,* which in part would lead me not only to Spain but to the author's other work "The Short Happy Life of Francis Macomber" and the Cape buffalo that is a pivotal element to the plot. Years later, again by the sea, I made the acquaintance of my white-bearded idol, but this time in person. How clearly I remember that evening in 1959 when Ernest Hemingway and I sat on rickety chairs at a lopsided table, its legs sinking unevenly into coarse damp sand that skirted the Malaga Bay. There, until four in the morning I sat entranced, listening to my hero speak of many things, among them the buffalo that he had admired, killed, and later returned to life in ink.

So, at Ololasurai I decided that if Cape buffalo, except for the cloven marks they left in the mud or the nests they bent in the grass on the hillside, did not come within view of our camp, we would go to them.

On either side of the tent rested two skulls from bulls that had been pulled down by lions. With great black twists of horn and textured boss crowning the sharp angles and smooth circles of sun-parched bone, a Cape buffalo skull has a certain static, hard, stylized design of powerful aesthetic appeal. The most impressive of our camp decorations, one which had a forty-six-inch-wide sweep of horn, came from an animal that had been ambushed by four lions below the prehistoric caves. That lions attack and kill buffalo is evidenced again and again in areas where the two cohabit. That buffalo kill lions is an equal truth, but one which has seldom been seen, and never been photographed. Once, on the plain, I spied two lionesses feeding on a zebra colt they had brought down. With them were three cubs barely old enough to walk. The sun was minutes from setting when, almost finished with their meal, both cats raised their crimsoned whiskers, and I swung the binoculars in the direction they were looking. Approaching us were three mature bull buffalo who had gotten the scent of the cats by the same wind that partly played in my favor.

Nostrils tilted upward and dilated eyes straining to show white triangles at their inner edges, the buffalo halted while focusing on the lionesses. Then, shoulder to shoulder, they moved forward until they arrived at the zebra carcass. Meanwhile, the lionesses had disappeared into grass. There seemed no possibility, however, that the small, weak cubs could be more than a few yards away from where the aggressors then stood. In unison, the buffalo began to violently hook and charge about, scattering the air golden with seed heads that were shaken from the tall grass. I feared for the cubs, who seemed certain to have been left behind. After trampling the vegetation into a mat, the bulls, almost lost in the darkness, plodded off toward the river. What happened to the cubs, we would never know.

Another lion, I was told by a naturalist friend, had been less fortunate in escaping the rage, horns, and hooves of Cape buffalo. My friend had been watching six bachelor lions resting on a rise somewhere in the Serengeti. Suddenly, all of the cats rose, not bothering to stretch, and loped off, followed by my friend in a Land-Rover. A half mile away, lions and vehicle stopped at a herd of milling buffalo, some of which promptly charged the pride members and drove them away. In the center of the herd lay a male lion gasping for breath, eyes shut. My friend assumed that the buffalo, en masse, had run down the lion and would have gored and trampled it had not the rest of the pride appeared, along with the Land-Rover. With the vehicle, my friend was able to restrain the buffalo from finishing off the lion, who, when the sun set, still lay unconscious as his breathing faded.

Kay Turner told me that in the Serengeti, buffalo were responsible for more human injuries and deaths than those caused by any of the other big five: lion, elephant, rhinoceros, leopard. Actually, hippopotamuses and crocodiles liquidate greater numbers of people than do lions, leopards, or elephants. When in the security of the herd, Cape buffalo, like fighting bulls, will most often flee even from the hand waving of a small child. Alone, when insecurity ignites their rage, they are among the world's most dangerous creatures. Bulls that have been thrown out of the herd frequently establish territories which they guard against intruders. If these animals have suffered spear wounds or are bothered by ear or throat parasites, they can be especially dangerous. Few human victims of buffalo attack live to describe the horror of the happening. I not only know one who did, but was part of the Loita nightmare during my previous trip in which I thought for sure I had lost my friend and former assistant Joe Saccoman. The following account was later written by Saccoman as he lay in bed with a broken back:

"As we were on the return walk of a foot safari into the Loita Hills, Daniel, our Maasai guide, was in the lead. Dr. Bill Wheeler was second in line, Robert Vavra was third, and I followed him. Because hunting is illegal in Kenya, the only weapons that could be brought were the spears and semi swords carried by the five Maasai porters who followed behind us.

"With a bellow, a dark mass blurred foliage to our right, as Daniel's arm coiled back, then stretched forward to lance a spear. The others ran for the trees on the far side of the grass corridor. It seemed shorter to me to run diago-nally away from the bull, along the same side of the forest from which he had charged. The Cape buffalo singled me out, and when I reached the edge of the forest, we were face to face, separated by a clump of wrist-sized saplings, none of which were large enough to climb.

"He charged, and I moved, keeping the slight barrier of trees between us. As he bellowed furiously, my eyes focused on his as I sidestepped back and forth, then ran around the slight stand of saplings. My adrenaline was almost gone. [Joe had been sick and vomiting most of the night before and was barely in shape for the walk out of the forest.] I was exhausted. The buffalo stopped for a moment. I was dazed, wondering what I was doing in front of this monster. The voice of Kununga, who had been Bill's and my guide in Tanzania on the safari to Olmoti and Empakaai, came back to me: 'If you are on the ground, lie flat—very dangerous. If he gets you up, he will tear you apart with his horns, that is, if with his boss and hooves he hasn't already pounded and trampled your lungs and guts into bits. Sometimes, after a man is dead, the buffalo, not satisfied, will go down, and with one shoulder, flatten the human pulp into the ground until, except for bits of bone, it is almost undistinguishable from the mud.'

"'Got to get away,' I thought.

"'Someone throw a spear,' screamed Bill from across the clearing.

"The bull backed two steps into the forest and I dashed off toward the ghost of my friend's voice. Halfway across the clearing, my legs tied up and I fell, face first, sliding on my palms. The bull ran over me, but he was too close to have time to lower his horns. He swept by and circled back as I scrambled to my feet. Coming from behind he hammered me forward five more yards. I landed on my feet running, but he hit me again. I tumbled, sprawled fifteen feet from the tree in which my friends had taken refuge.

"A split second after I stopped rolling, there was a pounding on my chest. Then my whole body felt it was being crushed. I saw a mass of black horn boss and eyes a foot from mine. My senses blurred as, bellowing and grunting, he smashed me. Deep pain flashed through my back. Each crushing blow white-washed my sense—and still he kept ramming me. Was he slicing me with his horns?

"Only seconds had passed, but time slowed as my body went into shock, and it seemed that the buffalo had been on top of me forever. There was no way to get him off. He weighed two thousand pounds, I one hundred and sixty. Something warm was soaking me. I saw blood pouring everywhere, but in the storm of the attack I couldn't tell if it was mine or his. How much longer could I survive? I thought that I heard a distant scream, then realized that it was my own voice—going farther and farther away.

"I started giving in to death as the buffalo thrashed me again. Then I was alone.

"There was an instant of quiet before I heard Robert shouting. Rolling my body to the left, I saw that he had jumped out of the tree and was advancing, frantically waving his arms and madly shouting to decoy the animal, which was looking away from me and at him. 'Get back up here!' Bill Wheeler screamed at Robert from somewhere above. 'We can't have two dead men!'

"The buffalo charged Robert and ran him around the tree twice. As the bull came by the second time, it stopped ten feet from me and stared, again looking into my eyes. Slowly, I reached back to untangle my left foot from a bush.

"'Hold still. Don't move,' monotoned Robert, hardly moving his lips as he saw me reaching.

"I slowly lay flat again, watching the Cape's wild eyes, praying that he would leave me alone.

"Robert waved and yelled and again the buffalo turned, charging after him around the trunk several more times, and then it stopped. What could my friend do next? I wondered. How could he keep the buffalo from coming back to me and still save his own life?

"Suddenly, a Maasai, seated high in the tree, threw a camera bag, which hit the bull and caused it to whirl and pound at the canvas case.

"'Come, Joe!' Robert shouted, knowing that he could not reach me without bringing the bull into both of us. 'Now, Joe,' he encouraged, as Bill, from his perch, dropped a sixty-pound duffle bag onto the buffalo, which it tossed ten feet into the air, as if the sack were a feather pillow.

"I freed my leg from the bush and lunged as best I could toward the trunk. Robert had his arms around me, lifting me as Bill pulled from above.

"Once Robert had climbed into the tree fork next to me, a nauseous feeling flooded my insides. I collapsed against him, his arm around my chest, our toes not more than a foot above the bull's horns, which were now bashing at the tree trunk. Its great rolled black eyes were fixed on us, as with each charge we were splattered with blood, which oozed from around the broken spear shaft in its shoulder. I coughed and Robert told me to spit into his hand. The mucus was red.

"Internal injuries or puncture wounds, I thought.

"The bull came back to the trunk and grunted, straining his eyes upward, but his tremendous weight restricted his horns from reaching us. I was suddenly sick and threw up, spattering his horns.

"In the top of our tree was a Maasai warrior, then Bill, and below him Robert, holding me. The five other Maasai had climbed trees behind us, out of sight.

"There was a sudden terrible pain in my back, and it hurt to sit up.

"From his perch above, the Maasai shook the top of a small sapling, and the buffalo charged the movement of its trunk, then, bellowing deeply, spun in the opposite direction. There he stood, statue-like, as if waiting for his next victim. I could see the deep lines of the tendons in his cheeks and brow.

"'Do something, Daniel! Throw a spear! Please do something!' yelled Bill and Robert. Daniel and the others were still hidden from sight behind us in tall trees. 'We've got a man dying up here! Do something! Joe's dying!' pleaded Bill.

"No reply.

"The bull grunted again and turned his head to the base of our tree to slam his horns against the trunk, blood speckling our boots with each charge. I tried to pull myself up higher into the tree. My back was buckling.

"'I feel like I'm passing out. Can you hold me tighter?' I asked Robert. I thought I was going—dying. So did Robert, for, though his words and face expressed encouragement, his eyes started to moisten.

"'We've got to build him a frame,' said Bill, 'before he passes out.' He pointed to a limb beside the Maasai. 'That one,' he commanded, making a chopping motion with his hand to the warrior.

"They slid a series of limbs under me for support. It must have been three o'clock, and an hour had passed when now the crackling sound of fire moved in behind us, along the corridor of dry grass. But it was inhibited from reaching us by the green vegetation of the forest. [The fire had been set in a dry, grassy clearing a quarter of a mile away by Maasai, who, Daniel had told me, were trying to clear the area of mamba and cobra which had been killing their cattle.] Smoke seeped through the forest, discoloring the sun spots on leaves.

"'You've got to help us!' called Bill and Robert in desperation to the Maasai out of sight.

"'We don't have any spears left!' came Daniel's reply.

"Two more branches were slid beneath me. Twenty minutes later the buffalo walked ten yards away from us, after which the strongest of the Maasai, under the cover of thick vegetation, came from behind and threw his retrieved spear seventy-five feet in an unerring arc. The blade struck the bull high behind the shoulder, sinking three feet into its side.

"'It wasn't low enough, Daniel! It wasn't low enough! You'll have to throw another spear!' shouted Robert.

"'We don't have any more!' yelled Leparan, Daniel's nephew.

"The bull walked thirty feet farther away, probably trying to escape the fire which crackled ever louder, and dropped to its knees.

"'He's down!' yelled Bill. 'There's a spear right below us.'

"'Do it now, Leparan!' shouted Robert. 'He's down. Go around behind and cut the tendons. Hamstring him. Hurry, before he gets up!'

"Leparan stalked behind the bull and hamstrung it with his sword, then lodged the final killing spear in the bull's heart.

"Six Maasai lowered me down from the tree, the bend of my left arm pulling hard on Daniel's neck as I tried to ease the pain in my back. We had been in the tree for more than an hour and a half. They laid me on a blanket in the clearing.

"'We'll have to drive him to Nairobi,' said Bill, as he

pressed his fingers against my distorted spine, then pulled off my bloody shirt. 'Can't call the air doctors. Sometimes takes them twenty hours to deliver.' He took off his glasses and rubbed his eyes. 'You can't imagine how hard I was praying in that tree.'

"With five Maasai, Bill left for the Land-Rover in a run that would take them three hours. Robert stayed behind with me. The nightmare continued until sometime between midnight and dawn when we at last reached Nairobi where my injury was diagnosed by Dr. Alberto Bencivienga as a compression fracture of the L1 vertebra. The ability to control my intestines was also compromised by blood and swelling surrounding the injury. Eight seats were removed from a Pan Am jumbo so that I could be flown to London, and then California, where it will take another six months to determine whether or not back surgery is needed."

If Joe Saccoman had died, my interest in Cape buffalo would have gone with him and forever saddened my existence. But he did survive that Loita attack as did I, which brought to my interest in buffalo a rare dimension, a closeness which no nightmare or dream could have achieved. That experience had made me feel alive as I had never before felt alive.

It also made me feel other things. Later, people would ask questions about my actions. What do I remember most about Joe's near death? In the days prior to those moments of terror in Loita, I recall insisting on searching for Cape buffalo in the reserves while my friends quite naturally wanted to watch and photograph lions and elephants. Then we went on the foot safari into the Forest of the Lost Child. There was a bellow and crash of branches. I was running to save my life, fearful of being gored in seconds and crushed into nothingness. Somehow I climbed a tree

and was looking down at the mass of blood-splattered buffalo lashing at Joe, pounding him into the ground. In an instant he would be dead—already he was probably dying. His eyes were opened so very wide, startled by his own approaching annihilation. Then came his scream which was not an attempt to summon help or detour the animal. His shriek announced the ending of his life. That high-pitched death howl expressed the utter futility and horror of the happening as he listened to his own voice seemingly for the last time.

Several clear thoughts flashed through the blackness of my mind. I had to try to save Joe even though it seemed I would die in the act. Staying in the tree, immune to the awful howl of my friend's approaching extinction, was an impossibility. In those ever so brief seconds, my mind bizarrely projected a scene from the film The Macomber Affair, in which the dead Francis Macomber, on a stretcher covered by a blanket, is carried from a plane. Just before I jumped to the ground, I apologized to my widowed, aging mother, "I'm sorry, Muv." If I felt anything at that instant, it was more sadness than fright, sadness for her and for me, because I was not ready to die. As I slid from the branch, it was clear that if there existed the slightest chance of survival for Joe—and for me—neither my body or mind could be incumbered by fear.

Once my feet touched the ground, thoughts of death were gone. Never before, I believe, has my concentration been so intensely acute as I focused on living and how to continue doing so. Without question, years spent in association with Spanish fighting cattle, of having caped animals at ranch testings, determined much of what I thought and did. As I stepped forward and shouted to attract its attention, the buffalo raised its head from Joe. Then I waved my arms to provoke a charge. As the bull crashed after me and then circled the tree in pursuit, my greatest concern was not to trip over the network of wrist-sized roots that coiled the ground.

Suddenly the bull stopped on the opposite side of the trunk and swung his head in the direction of Joe, who was trying to untangle his boot from a vine. With a whisper I told my friend to be still, then I moved to the far side of the trunk to provoke another charge. The buffalo saw the movement and ran me around the tree. Again we both stopped, he on one side of the trunk, I on the other. He was still and so was I. At that instant it seemed the only life in the forest was the contact between our eyes, three feet apart, separated by the V of the tree trunk. One thing could be seen in those large pale-blue, brown-rimmed irises, which bulged and strained to expose widening triangles of white at their outer edges: I saw in that stare the utter need and obsession—for whatever motive—to kill, destroy, and rid the forest and world of me. It was as though I didn't belong there, which in part was true. The buffalo had no option but to eliminate me.

Blood bubbled up from the broken spear shaft in the bull's sparsely haired black side. I wondered if the glistening red that colored the horn tips had come from the animal's own wound or from Joe. Short blasts of breath struck my face with strong smells of chewed grass. Threads of silver saliva burst from the glistening muzzle to spatter my forehead and cheeks.

In those moments, these were the most conscious of my feelings. Later in the tree, holding Joe in my arms, his spine distorted, my hand splashed with the blood he had just spit into it, I looked up at Dr. Wheeler, who shook his head in a sign of no hope. Minutes later, when the body in my arms started to go limp, I felt terribly cheated. It was not fair that on the ground I had saved Joe only to have him now, safely in the tree, die in my arms. We had been

through enough, damn it. Why could we not simply be back in Nairobi with Joe alive under clean hospital sheets?

An hour and a half later, the buffalo was finally dead and we were on the ground. Another hour passed before a small Japanese field vehicle, loaded with Maasai, crashed into the clearing from the roadless forest. In his dash for our own Land-Rover, Bill had met these men and sent them after us. It was simply unfortunate to have no choice but to have to double up Joe to fit him into the cramped rear section of that automobile, knowing that the slightest movement might paralyze him from the waist down. But better to have his lower body go forever limp in this forest, I felt, than to have all of him die from the smashed liver and spleen that we suspected he had suffered. It was simply bad luck when halfway to our destination, the vehicle veered to a stop with a tire puncture. So they could remove the spare, I had to unload Joe, stretch him out on the ground while the tire was replaced, then lift and double him back into those cramped quarters.

When we met Bill at an enkang an hour away, and began preparing a bed in the Land-Rover for Joe, I made the driver of the other vehicle promise to wait for us. Only he knew how to lead us out of the miles of roadless forest and onto the dirt track that led from Loita. It was simply bad luck again when at last ready to leave, with less than an hour of light left in the sky, we learned that the other driver had gone on without us. It was almost as annoying when, still an hour from that road, Daniel wanted to abandon us. Who gave a damn about the lions and buffalo about which he complained, as he and I ran before the Land-Rover, trying to guide Bill away from hyena and warthog holes. I had only one fear, that we would become stuck in one of them and that Joe would stop breathing before we could get him to Nairobi.

What bad luck, I thought each time we came to a stream and had to turn back, or a boulder or a fallen log or a place where the forest was too thick. Suddenly the Land-Rover grated to a stop behind us, its underside caught up on a grass-covered stump. Bill jumped out and we pushed and pulled and rocked the vehicle, Joe moaning inside, until at last it slid free. By then the light was almost gone. Did bloody Daniel actually have any idea where we were? Fifteen minutes after the sun set, we found the semblance of a track that led down the escarpment. Relieved at last to be out of the roadless forest, we had been driving about twenty minutes when a tremendous banging came from underneath the Land-Rover as it appeared to drop onto its very frame. While precious minutes and Joe's life seemed to be ticking away, Bill climbed out and with a torch crawled the red earth beneath the vehicle to find a spring hanging loose, ripped from its place of support. Continuing down the deeply eroded track, the car's body banged without pause against the axle. With each bump along that seemingly endless descent, Joe sighed or moaned in pain, my hand on his forehead or holding his hand. If he was dying, we could not let him feel alone.

Just past Narok, he sighed, "Robert, can you cover me with more blankets? I'm shaking, I feel so cold." What sort of insanity was this? Where was I? How could this be? The words were identical to those I had heard a month past, but now they were in English, not those heard in Spanish at more or less the same hour near midnight. Where was I?

On a bumpy road to Nairobi with a dying friend or in that shabby clinic in Northern Spain with a seemingly dying matador short miles from the seaside *plaza de toros* where he had been tossed and trampled by his second bull. There, the immediate diagnosis had been a broken neck. As I held Joe's hand or put my hand on his forehead, so I had done just a month ago in those still hours near midnight with my matador friend.

In that grubby, stifling, practically abandoned Spanish clinic I had dozed off in the chair beside the bed when my friend's voice brought me from sleep and back into that nightmare. "*Viejo,*" he had whispered weakly. "Something's happening to me. My legs are so cold. I can barely feel my feet. I'm so cold. *Viejo,* cover me with more blankets." And then he had started to shake as it seemed sure he was going away forever. There I had shouted and raged until a nun had rushed from the emptiness of that pueblo clinic and out into the blackness to try to find a doctor. Here in the Land-Rover with Joe, only Bill and the night would have heard my pleas, "Do something, damn it! He's dying!"

Our African nightmare ended several days later in Nairobi, as I stood alone, watching a Pan Am jumbo jet carry Joe and Bill upward, becoming smaller and smaller on its way to London and Los Angeles. When I left the airport I went to the farm of Karen Blixen. Alone with my thoughts, as dusk fell, I sat outside of the house at the millstone table and watched the Ngong Hills absorbed by the evening grayness. How wrong I had been in thinking that we had such bad fortune in Loita. Unfortunate? No. We had been so, so lucky.

Now, several years later, deciding to go after buffalo on foot at Ololasurai, I questioned this seemingly suicidal craving. Why? If anything I wanted to live and had never experienced such joy in existence as I felt at this camp in the Kenyan Highlands. I suppose, in part, I was motivated by a difficult-to-explain, mystical attraction to Cape buffalo. To me, they and Africa

were practically one and the same. However, the Loita experience, instead of creating an aversion, had provided another addiction, that of the adrenaline rush which came from being on foot and close to the buffalo "of the serene marble brow." Only then did I truly sense that I was in the Africa of all those books that had made my middle-class American childhood so wondrous.

So, at Ololasurai, in the daylight absence of buffalo around camp, late one evening we dispatched two warriors in search of them.

At the first rose-colored light of dawn, one of the buffalo scouts sprinted past our still smoldering fire. Hours earlier, six bachelor bulls had been sighted feeding knee-deep in a marsh, slurping up the mud with every sucking step as horns glistened under the soon-to-disappear moon.

At considerable distance, the youths had followed until the bulls, just before the sun had started bleaching the sky, moved to high ground, taking cover in a nasty expanse of thornbush. While one boy scaled an acacia to keep watch, the other had run five miles to us.

Sekerot saddled the mares and we set off at a trot, the hunter, spear in hand, in the lead and Morkau just behind the horses' tails. Once free of the stream's saplings and tangles, my heels touched the black mare into canter. Zebra galloped off, angling to gaze not only at the unfamiliar equines, but at the men on their backs. Impala fled in soaring leaps. Topi stampeded by, rouge-slate flashes through a lattice of thorn, and ahead, giraffe loped from the horizon more as if to escape the rising sun than us.

A mile from where the buffalo now rested, unaware of our plan, and of being watched, the horses were left in Morkau's care while we continued on foot. Then the lone acacia tree rose above the thorn, a Maasai high in its branches, through which the sun was now gleaming. A whispered exchange of words between the scout and Sekerot had less meaning to my ears than did the breeze that slightly swayed the acacia leaves to communicate the wind was in our favor.

"He says the six bulls have taken cover and have laid up there," Sekerot whispered, indicating a basin two hundred yards away which overflowed with thickets of thorn.

"Shall we go?" I questioned, squinting toward the inhospitable divisions of bush as I thought, "After Loita, why push your luck?"

"Too many of us will frighten them," replied Sekerot. "If you want to get really close to them, you and he should go right now—alone." He pointed at a hazel-eyed youth, the shorter of the scouts who stood, spear in hand, gazing not too happily in the direction of the invisible buffalo.

"Me, alone," I thought.

"Hurry, if you are going, but take care. In that cover you may not see their horns until you are on top of them. Go, if you are going," he urged. Given ten seconds more, reason would have cemented me to the acacia's shadow.

"All right," I whispered and, almost at a run, followed the red cloth and spear ahead which marked our path through thorns that menaced from either side. A stream stopped the boy, whose downcast eyes read messages in its murky flow. He pointed at saucer-sized, cloven furrows, into which water was still seeping.

Scurrying along a narrow corridor of grass that cut through the labyrinth of thorn, I was filled with both panic and cool calculation as I looked for a tree trunk, anything to climb. But there was nothing except the network of fine-branched thorned domes, twelve feet high and in circumference, each twig of which was spiked with two-inch needles. If escape was needed, here it could not be found.

The crash came exactly as it had in Loita, except now it sounded from behind. The bull did not bellow. No one heaved a spear. And instead of charging straight on, the horns thrust off to side-angle behind us as we sprinted to catch a three-quarter view of a muddied shoulder, back, and boss, thirty feet away, rampaging off through the scrub.

In seconds, Sekerot, seemingly shaken, sword in hand, was beside us. Between deep breaths, his words came. "From the tree we saw you walking and them sleeping, neither aware of the other. Do you know how close you were to that one?" he questioned, his face tense. "You walked right past him, ten meters away, before he awoke and charged. You were out of sight and he was unable to locate you. The wind was still favorable."

"We were really that close?" I questioned, as Sekerot guided us to the thicket of bent grass scattered with dung, where the bull had been resting. "And if you still don't trust me," he smiled, "look at his spear." He pointed at the hazel-eyed boy's blade, which was trembling as if grasped by a palsied hand.

That afternoon, back in camp, I sat transcribing notes, when Sekerot, smiling in the present while making a joke of the past, asked, "Are you writing about this morning?" I nodded. "And do you want the name of the boy who accompanied you into the thorn?" Again I nodded. "This time I can only give you a clue," came the reply. "He wrote *Hamlet*."

During the daylight hours, danger at Ololasurai was not the lone male lion that leapt the stream behind the tent, leaving his calling card stamped in mud, or the herd of elephants which cracked branches covering the water with a mosaic of green leaves. Danger was the lioness with cubs who dozed until a man approached so closely that when she suddenly awoke to find flight distance invaded, attack seemed the only alternative, even though she would have preferred to flee. Danger also was the cow elephant slumbering, suckling calf at her side, curtained in olive less than a quarter mile downstream from the tent. Unaware of her presence, Morkau, jabbering with a friend, approached the stand of trees. Suddenly, a mass of gray movement blurred behind the vegetation as the cow rushed out to catch his friend, trying to pancake him into the ground with her forehead. Great clods of earth fell on fleeing Morkau's brow as the cow lashed up her tusks. Somehow, both men escaped.

However, the greatest danger while the sun still shone on Ololasurai was an easily gained sense of false security that came from rarely seeing the predators themselves. Scat, pug marks, and reports of slaughtered calves and goats were not as frightening as being brought up short by hard pupils and gleams of yellow, accompanied by a black tail tip lashing in the grass several arm's lengths away. That predators were around us could not be doubted from the secondhand evidence of their presence. That they would show themselves in broad daylight was yet another story.

Even around the campfire, while warming hands or joking with friends, one was reminded of the often forgotten terror that twilight could settle on Ololasurai. Its voice came in short apprehensive yelps and almost melodious yodels from some Maasai who, through necessity or carelessness, found himself far from home when darkness fell. With seldom-heard vocalizations, he was attempting to frighten a waiting lion or leopard from the same path which, under the sun, had heard his carefree whistling.

During the six months before I arrived, lions had reportedly killed five humans near Ololasurai. One had been a small girl, who, alone at dusk, was cooking some maize porridge in a corral next to her mother's hut when a lioness sprang upon her. Not even bothering to leave the enkang, the hungry cat carried the child to an empty sheep enclosure. While the Maasai family searched the countryside, the girl was eaten in their home. Just below camp, a Maasai, drunk and without a torch, had stumbled along the path trailed by a lion. The cat then, circling ahead, waited for its victim at a stream crossing, killed him there, and had that meal under a thornbush. Five prostitutes, who had been selling themselves to park rangers at the Mara, were evicted from the reserve by the warden. Dumped at the gate in late afternoon, they foolishly decided not to wait for a bus, but to start walking to Narok with the hope of catching a ride along the way. When darkness was near, a pride of curious lions began following the girls, who senselessly broke into a run. Two of them were able to save themselves by climbing trees, from which they watched their companions hideously devoured.

However, these stories and the Ololasurai night did not restrict us to the warmth and safety of the campfire, even if predators were on the prowl. I had with me a cassette tape of hyena and lion calls, which we used to entertain us away from the tent not only on nights of full moon, but also those of total darkness.

Once, shortly before midnight, Sekerot, Sicona, and I took a rotten leg of goat, one salvaged at the lower enkang from a leopard's only partly successful attack, and carried it a mile upstream. As we moved along, our raised spears jabbed up and down at the full moon, which provided light to guide our way. When the scent had been spread around the expanse of the clearing by dragging the bait in narrowing circles, we tied it to a tree limb, low enough to be enticing, but high enough to prevent the first hyena from snatching it.

After we had climbed twenty feet into the fork of an adjoining acacia, I turned on the tape recorder to fill the night with hyena voices strange to the highly territorial local residents. Few seconds passed before answers came from all directions, and in minutes eight to ten high-shouldered, low-hipped bodies appeared against the silver of the moonlit clearing. In the faint light we watched as one hyena after another leapt for the bait, like sharks lunging upward from the deep to flash the darkness with their empty fangs. Finally, before one hyena, larger than the rest, reached the meat and tore it from the rope, we ignited our bright torches to focus on his companions, the sudden flashes of light dropping them from view like mechanical ducks at a carnival shooting gallery.

On the night of a waning moon, we took the tape cassette to some distance in front of the tent and, after dragging the head of a sheep round the forked clearing where the two streams joined, we climbed a tree and blasted out recorded sounds of lions feeding. Hyenas answered. One ran under our tree, then back and forth, three times unable to locate the kill from which the noise was coming. Shortly thereafter, two jackals circled the tree where the bait was tied. As the moon came and went behind marbled clouds, we heard the muffled pounding of heavy feet on wet grass and soil. "What could it be?" my eyes questioned Sekerot. Hooves against earth did not make those sounds. There was a distant blur coming full out, emerging from heavy bush, and in seconds the shape took the form of the largest black-maned lion I had ever seen. He came spread out at a full run, directly toward our tree, and passed, looking for a kill that did not exist, six feet beneath our dangling toes.

A moonless night took us to the plain, searching for gazelle. Finding a cluster of them feeding with zebra, I flashed our most powerful torch in the eyes of the nearest buck, then twenty yards away. Slowly, I stepped closer, placing my feet with care while keeping the beam targeted on the gazelle's blinded stare. He did not move. Finally, a yard away, I reached out and touched a soft flank, to send him bounding off into the blackness. Turning off the torch, I stood for a moment alone in the night, savoring the joy of that gentle touch.

One afternoon the smell of the rain was in the air when two Maasai appeared against the darkening sky. Like others who passed by the tent, they were sure to be scouting for grazing, avoiding the plains below Olololasurai, which were being devastated by armies of antelope and zebra. The migration's course would take it partly through the reserve before crossing the swollen Mara River. There thousands of wildebeest would be swept or pushed under the current, lungs filled with muddy water, bodies soon floating like bloated wineskins. Finally, caught up on some branch, the shore, or on an island of stone, these carcasses provided nourishment for crocodiles, vultures, and monitor lizards. Once I watched a hippopotamus, who, seemingly enraged by the bloated, rotten cadavers that polluted his water home, seized the floating bodies as they passed, pulling them out of sight under the river's surface. Then, shooting

upward in a great surge of foam, he shook the wildebeest in his great jaws until the most rotten were dismembered, limbs scattering in all directions.

Depleted grazing was not the Maasai's only reason for coming our way. Of like concern were the hosts of predators who followed such migrations and would just as soon have cow or sheep for supper as wildebeest, though lions seemed especially fond of the fatty meat of zebra.

"Do you know that where you were hunting butterflies along the stream this morning, over your footprints are the pug marks of a large male lion?" came Sekerot's voice from inside the tent. "I found where he lay in the grass on the bank and watched you pass. Last night two goats were taken from the lower enkang. It was the leopard that passes the tent. Moseka will have to take more care with the horses."

Shortly after three the next morning, roars brought me awake. The lions, I calculated, were ten minutes downstream. Sekerot slept soundly. Five minutes passed. Again the lions announced their presence, approaching closer to camp. The hushed voices of Moseka and Morkau, coupled with the uneasy stomping of the mares, could now be heard. Next came a series of blasting roars that seemed to sound from just outside the tent, enveloping it like the echoed rumbling of an afternoon storm, though, in fact, the lions were still one hundred yards away. What made me anxious was the safety of the mares, not our own. Generally, the mere netting and canvas of a tent will prevent lions from bothering people—out of sight, out of mind. Once on the plain, though, as I slept on the ground, I felt more than casual concern when two male lions engaged in full battle, circled, roared, and rampaged so closely around our canvas refuge that their lashing paws strummed the guy lines of the tent.

"Sekerot," I whispered. "Sekerot." He stirred as I raised my voice. "Lions. Lions." Torch in one hand, the other unzipping the mosquito-netted door flap, my friend disappeared in a second to become no more than a faint shadow through the canvas of the tent. He and Moseka threatened the lions first with shouts, and then more strongly with beams of light, which generally are enough to frighten away lions in the night.

The roaring ceased, and not until we were back in bed did a single call come from upstream, where the lions later killed a cow. Now calm, the horses Katie and Narok nickered softly from the corral, quieted by Moseka's Loita lullaby. Poor Narok. Little time would pass before the lions would return, though now unannounced as Moseka slept, wrapped in a blanket, at the entrance to the prickly-thorn enclosure. A scruffy-maned male was the first to crash through the woven acacia branches, and before Sicona could spear it in the side, my favorite mare lay dead with her black neck broken.

On horseback, Sekerot and I explored the hills around camp, Moseka or Morkau leading on foot, spear-cutting the air, entrusted with detecting lion, elephant, or Cape buffalo in the thick cover through which we often passed. None of the Maasai who crossed our path had ever seen a horse. Most women and children ran away from our "strange" beasts to gaze back in both wonderment and apprehension. More impressive was an entry into a Maasai settlement, people fleeing before the mares' approach, as the Aztecs surely scattered in the path of Cortez.

Now and then we sighted recently circumcised youths. They appeared alone or in numbers, shrouded black and haloed with the bodies of half a hundred stuffed birds fashioned and supported with sticks into sinister-looking headdresses. The feathered halos were a display of recently acquired manhood. These in kera oo motonyi, or bird boys as we called them, could be seen static on a distant rise, headdresses moving slightly in the wind against puffy cumulus or clustered together at the coolness of a stream. Often they sang in celebration of one life left behind and a new one entered, while one of the group, with hardened feet and long slim calves, propelled himself straight up into the air. At the pinnacle of this leap, the dancer, as if only pausing in his upward voyage, would vibrate his shoulders while rapidly bobbing his head to and fro, before descending to join his companions on the ground.

The behavior of these boys, as all Maasai life, was governed by a code, variation from which never crossed the mind. For example, bird boys must enter the enkang before the cattle are corralled each evening. If they arrive after this happening, several animals must be removed, allowing the boy to enter, followed by the reentry of cows or bulls. When bird boys come to a stream or pond, they must tear up grass, spit on it before dropping it to the water's surface. When thirsty, they are restricted from drinking water unless it has been first cleansed with milk, which is of an importance in Maasai life that the stranger can barely comprehend. Milk is the most valued of gifts. It is food and the source of existence, unlike maize, cabbage, or meat, which are merely objects one puts in one's mouth for perhaps a pleasurable taste.

If it rains, bird boys cannot take cover underneath a tree or umbrella. When a storm catches them outside their enkang, they may walk to their house, never run, in search of shelter. Looking into a mirror is of the greatest taboo. If they are attacked by a buffalo or predator, taking refuge in a tree is not permitted. Food may not be consumed unless it is eaten in a hut. In the house before traveling, they are given a cup of milk wrapped in grass. When darkness falls, they remove the headdress and hang it in the hut's 195 doorway, restricted from leaving the corral until daybreak. They cannot eat or see food touched or belonging to a circumcised man, and can take it only from a woman's hands. If meat is eaten, it must be cut by a woman, never the diner. Bathing with water is prohibited, and cleaning one's dirty body can be done only with cow dung, boiled maize, or cattle urine. Bird boys are restricted from having sex with circumcised girls. (After their first menstruation, all girls undergo a clitorectomy.) They may not sleep in a hut unless the female owner is present, and never in the presence of circumcised males other than their age-mates—not even their fathers. They cannot wash their clothes. Normally, boys live under these restrictions, unbathed and dressed in black and headdressed, for five or six months, though one youth was said to roam around our camp, his ragged feathered halo fluttering in the wind, for a year and a half. With the bird boys' growing sense of manly worth blossoms an arrogance almost without parallel. This period in their lives ends when their heads are shaved in a formal ceremony, cleansing the way to the Maasai heaven on earth—that of the moran—the warrior. However, with the Kenyan government's attempts to homogenize the people of its forty-some main tribes, one sees fewer and fewer moran each year.

During these walks or rides in the highlands, warriors seldom crossed our paths, but those we did meet were unpredictable, arrogant, accustomed to having their own way and satisfied with little else—but more than anything, they were totally fascinating. Their behavior was also tightly scripted. In a reversal of their lives as bird boys, they now could sleep with all women, clitoris present or removed. They could not eat meat seen or touched by females, and if they did so, punishment came by having their clothing taken away. A toga could be

reclaimed only after begging forgiveness, and then collected solely by the hands of the warriors' mothers. In a house, warriors must drink milk in the presence of another warrior, but not until first offering to serve the friend. This cannot be done before the host, with a glowing ember, has inspected for cleanliness the interior of the calabash or gourd. When warriors attend meat feasts with uncircumcised girls (circumcised females are not allowed), the girls remove their skirts and, like moran, wear a mini version of the normal Maasai shuka, which exposes the nakedness of most of the body. Girls and men then display their physiques in like manner. However, warriors are not allowed to make love during the feast. If they do so, the meat consumed will bring ill fortune. Any warrior who does go off with a girl at this time, if caught, is beaten. On cattle raids (which today seldom take place) moran cannot kill women, girls, or very young boys. If they do so, they will be cursed. They should not journey alone, but always in the company of another warrior. If a warrior does travel without company, he may not drink milk, going hungry until he is in the presence of another moran.

The restrictions and rules listed here for newly circumcised boys and warriors merely scratch the surface of the code of behavior that governs the life of all Maasai. The life of women, while subservient as well as restricted, is somewhat less complicated than that of the Maasai male. These pages, however, do not pretend to explain Maasai tradition. They are merely a brief reflection of a way of life that I was able to glimpse during a very short time from our tent in Ololasurai. Even with Sekerot's articulate, patient, sensitive, lengthy explanations, Maasai code and thought would be almost as incomprehensible to me when I left Kenya as they had been the day I arrived there. Why the ways of the people of Maa had not before

been accurately documented, except recently, by Maasai themselves (i.e., Tepilit Ole Saitoti) or by the few outsiders (i.e., Cheryl Bentsen) whose minds were inquisitive and persistent enough to sift through the sometimes nebulous feedback that one receives from the Maasai mouth, I was able to understand. To take the most basic example of false starts in trying to piece together the Maasai puzzle: the misuse of the Maa language in Kenya is more readily explained when one is aware that most Maasai will rarely correct a nonmember of their race when he or she mispronounces or misuses a Maa word. This basic deterrent to communication was evidenced almost everywhere I set foot. Whether this confusion is prompted by a Maasai not wishing to impolitely confront a foreigner with his or her mistake or is the result of simply not caring, I am not sure. So, when the first white man set eyes on a Maasai warrior camp, a corral of thorn incorporating dung huts in its perimeter, he was correctly told, "That is a manyata." When the stranger visited another Maasai corral circled with huts and he referred to it as "manyata," his proclamation went uncorrected, even though a corral with dung dwellings inhabited by families, used for daily living and not built for special celebrations, is, without variation, in Maa, an enkang. A manyata is strictly a temporary Maasai settlement, erected and used during one of the many types of celebrations that are seemingly difficult to understand and explain but of maximum importance and can sometimes last a year before concluding. These traditional fiestas are hardly the simplified celebrations of marching bands and soda pop known to most of us. Again, as in everything Maasai, each minute act is dictated by a steadfast rule. That is why the people of Maa, though they may question and be confused about other topics, are unconsciously and absolutely certain of one thing: who they are—Maasai.

Such is this tradition of misused words that even white men who have lived most of their lives in Kenya, or were born there, use "manyata" as all-encompassing for every corral circled with huts. As if this were not enough, today Maasai themselves label signboards "manyatta" to announce permanent family settlements opened to paying tourists. Adding more vinegar to the wound, modern Maasai, ignoring their own tongue with even the improper use of "manyata," vary further by frequently employing the Swahili word "boma," which signifies any corral.

Another example of Maasai indifference to mispronunciation by the outsider could be illustrated by my own experience. When Ntiti (pronounced "Nteetee") first came to camp and I had Sekerot ask his name, it came out "Ntete" (pronounced "Ntehteh"), which was then what all of us, Maasai included, used to address him. Even when his semi-educated brother visited our tent to collect the school fee I had promised, he referred to his brother as "Ntete." Normally, another Maasai who mispronounced his brother's first name would have been corrected, but because Sekerot and Miton, our sometimes driver, wore Western clothes and spoke English, they may have been considered extensions of myself. It was not until the boys' mother visited camp and one day sat drinking tea outside the tent that Sekerot overheard her laughing with a female friend at how we mispronounced her son's name, concluding that "if they want to call him 'Ntete' instead of 'Ntiti,' then, for them, that shall be his name." This expresses perfectly the Maasai philosophy about such things.

Since returning to the past was impossible for our Maasai friends, in a small way I hoped to help several of them into their questionable future. Ntiti and Sameri, I was able to send to school. Kardasha was too old and traditional for that kind of education. So the only way it seemed I could make his life immediately better was to sponsor his circumcision, which was long overdue and therefore an embarrassment to him and his family. A recent drought and the loss of cattle had left Kardasha's father lacking funds for the ceremony. With the cutting of our friend's foreskin, I would became not only his second father, but symbolically the husband to his mother, which caused good-natured joking when I arrived at their enkang, three hours' walk from camp.

Upon assuming the responsibility for Kardasha's circumcision celebration, of least concern to me were items and services that could be paid for with coin: sugar, potatoes, cooking oil, kerosene, onions, honey, spices, wheat flour, the blanket for the man who would hold our friend during the operation, and the payment of one sheep to a man of the Ndorobo tribe who would perform the surgery. What did weigh heavily, however, was my friend and symbolic relative's behavior under the Ndorobo's knife, which would unmistakably reflect on a family that now included me. The boy's father had had little choice in his son's presence on earth, something that a passionate moment on the hard-skinned berth in a smoky hut had brought into existence. However, my own association with Kardasha was a matter of choice. If things went wrong, it would be said that I had bad judgment for having selected a coward for a son, one who called me by a special name, Ol chorelai.

One afternoon, Kardasha arrived at camp with a francolin and superb starling killed that morning, two more ornaments to add to his bird boy's headdress. When he bowed his head for my touch, as do all uncircumcised Maasai when greeting adults, and then sat near the fire delicately skinning his prizes, I studied his face. Was there any sign of nervousness to indicate that the most important moment of his life was three short days distant? Did anything in his countenance betray that the boy thought brave by all Ololasurai harbored feelings which would not surface until he felt, and maybe watched, a knife slicing the most delicate part of his body? Looking into his eyes, the whites of which at dusk were so clear that they almost seemed luminous, I reflected on what Sekerot had told me about Maasai circumcision.

At the pinnacle of a Maasai youth's life is the day his body takes on the physical appearance seen only in men and at which time he proves if he is one or not. Circumcision, which may occur anytime between the early teens and the mid twenties can become an all-consuming obsession: wanting to exchange the limited rights of childhood for the respect and freedom of being a man. Sekerot told me that when he was sixteen years of age and still uncircumsized, he was unable to stand the strain of feeling that he was already a man, though he was still being treated as a boy. Nearly out of his mind wanting that important day of circumcision to arrive, he dared tradition by bringing the cattle home from pasture at noon, instead of dusk. This was not only an open defiance to his father, but to every other elder at the enkang. Once in the corral, he stood in its center and shouted, "I am going to be circumcised, and if anyone thinks he can stop me, let him step out here and die!" This was unacceptable behavior from an uncut youth, but not a voice was raised from inside the smoky huts, not even that of his father, who, though angered, felt some pride in his son's sense of self-worth and determination. Not much time passed before Sekerot's day did come, when he showed such coolness under the blade that afterward warriors circled the corral with him proudly on their shoulders.

It was not enough for a boy to arrive at circumcision age and wish the act performed. Economics played a decided role in what took place or did not. Since circumcision is a celebration into manhood, and celebrations universally call for entertaining guests, this day would not arrive unless a boy's family could afford to throw a party, or Maasai bar mitzvah if one wished to think of it in those terms. Wealthy parents had no problem in dealing with massive "coming outs" attended by hundreds of guests who drank whole skins of beer and feasted on as many slaughtered sheep and cattle as they could consume. Poor families had to wait and wait, traveling great distances to unreceptive relatives in the hope of acquiring even the slightest financial support. Kardasha's family was one of these, and if I had not chanced along and taken a liking to them, who knows how long my friend would have had to wait, frustrated and ashamed, while boys much younger than he paraded about with bird headdresses, eyeing girls who soon would be their lovers. Kardasha's age could only be estimated at between eighteen and twenty-one, since few Maasai are aware of the day of their birth, at most, the season, and only sometimes the year. Our friend had collected forty-eight birds, which were concealed in a plastic bag, each delicately mummy-wrapped in cloth, prepared for a day that it seemed would never dawn.

For a youth to want the responsibility of an approaching circumcision is one thing, but acquiring it and quaking under its weight is another. As I watched Kardasha pick an acacia twig and, with his fingers, snap from it thorns which he was using to fix the francolin skin to a carved wooden mannequin, I thought of other brave men I knew who wished with all their hearts for a certain day to come

and, once it had arrived, questioned the outcome. In Spain few were my matador acquaintances who did not complain continually because of the difficulty of obtaining *corridas* and bulls to kill on the sand of a ring where they could perform not only for money and love of the act, but to show men whose hearts had never known the feeling what bravery was all about. However, once those young and not-so-young Spaniards had put their names to a contract, or several, then the worry became not "When will I fight?" but "Now I have to fight age-soured, overweight bulls of poor breeding, in a country ring where the infirmary, at best, is equipped with a wad of cotton and a bottle of iodine." I wondered if Kardasha likewise had misgivings about circumcision now that the approaching day would soon be reality.

More than bravery, to lie as if in sleep during one's own circumcision, without anesthetic, calls for the sheerest kind of concentration, and for this a Maasai passes his boyhood in preparation. Maasai children continually test themselves in shows of valor and concentration. The most obvious evidence of this are the self-inflicted burn marks that scar their upper thighs. Good enough is simply not to scream out under the Ndorobo's knife, for it is these mysterious, wily hunters who usually perform the task. Actually, Maasai know how to do the surgery, but feel the act unworthy of their station. Equally unattractive to them is metalwork, the making of spears and arrows, which is also left to the Ndorobos.

Early on the morning of the circumcision, once the initiate has bathed in a stream or pond, he returns to the enkang and sits on ground covered by a special hide. Directly behind him sits an older man, loins touching the boy's hips. The arms of this man, who is the holder, circle the boy's chest. Cold water is then poured over the initiate's scalp, which was shaved the day before.

In the hours and weeks previous to this moment, the boy is psyched up for his ordeal. Little may be said to a known coward, but if the initiate is thought to be brave, passersby and acquaintances, using reverse psychology, mock him, half teasing and half in dead seriousness. "You'll never sit still. You'll scream. You'll shake your fingers like a frightened girl. You'll stiffen your legs." And if this were not enough, the youth is most likely confronted by a nearly hysterical mother, who wails and moans, "Oh, I know you'll disgrace us. You'll flinch or cry out and mess yourself. I know it as I see you before me." Fathers seem to fear more for their own pride and reputation than for that of their sons—for after all, they are one and the same. Tormented at already having had to pass sixteen or eighteen years in terror of their own day of reckoning, these men now have to relive the entire experience. With their son's circumcision they are symbolically responsible for the finale of an act over which they exercise absolutely no control.

To the initiate, the list of contrary factors must seem endless. The Ndorobo will be given a goat or the equivalent of fifteen dollars for his services, not to mention the payment that will come his way if the boy reacts in the slightest to the knife. Will the wily little man of the forest prolong the operation and cut unnecessarily to make the boy flinch, in which case the surgeon will collect an additional sheep or steer?

So the boy is now sitting on the hide, icy water running down his forehead, the holder's arms loosely around his chest. People continue to cast doubt on the event. "I can see he's going to move. Watch that finger. Look at his eyes. He's about to blink." These remarks, however, are mostly drowned out by encouragement shouted from newly circumcised age-mates. By this time, the initiate is probably calmest of all. For the rest of the family, it seems the world is drawing to an end.

Then, just how does a coward show his color? In those brief seconds, what can cause shame to hang around the youth's neck through old age until hyenas are chewing at his bones? Several times when we visited enkangs, Sekerot and Miton, while smiling slightly, pointed out men my age and whispered, "He ran from the knife. That one moved a hand. The short one shit himself." As the Ndorobo's dirty fingers pull at the foreskin, dozens or perhaps hundreds of spectators strain their eyes, concentrating almost as much as the boy—they on his body, he out of it.

The initiate's hands should remain completely relaxed, fingers loosely spread. Arms must not show the slightest sign of tension. Toes cannot straighten or unnaturally curl. Feet should remain as they do while resting. Muscles of the calves and thighs may not contract in the slightest. The abdomen must not flex. Shoulders cannot pull back at the hint of a cut or until the Ndorobo has finished the job. And now, the face. The eyes may be directed straight ahead, at the surgeon's fingers and operation, cast on the ground, or remain completely closed. The lips must not purse or draw. But from whatever posture is assumed, from the start of the operation to the finish there can be no variation in the boy's attitude. The initiate should represent the embodiment of the calmest, deepest, most concentrated sleep, eyes opened or shut. Of course, to voice the slightest whimper is unforgivable. To mess oneself, beyond reproach. Though the procedure may not take more than two or three minutes, to those closely involved it lasts a lifetime as the surgeon makes seemingly infinite cuts on the figure that appears caught up totally in slumber. All this time, advice and criticism, though hardly heard above the bird boys' shouts of encouragement, streams from the crowd. "That cut is not clean. You've taken too much. You've not taken enough. Do it quicker. Don't pinch that boy unnecessarily."

Maasai circumcision is not the simple act of pulling forward the foreskin and cutting that which exceeds the head of the penis. Involved here is surgery in which only artistic achievement indicates a job well done.

What, then, if an initiate's fingers tremble, his lips tighten, or his eyes squint in acknowledgment of pain? If he "runs from the knife," shamed bird boy age-mates turn immediately and dash off, to be coaxed back by elders. The initiate and his parents may be spat upon by the crowd, who have the option of breaking the thorn fence to stampede the family's cattle and scatter them through the bush. Of least concern are the lost gifts of cows and goats that would have been the initiate's reward for bravery, or the fine paid to the Ndorobo. Most important is the label "coward," which indelibly marks a Maasai for the remainder of his existence.

On Monday, a report came from Kardasha's home. The beer was fermenting, and if not mature for Wednesday the day of the circumcision, yeast would be added. Those days brought anxiousness, like that aggravated by other waiting, as the happening progressed from faint thought in the back of my mind to the focus, on Monday evening, of everything I heard, spoke, or saw in my imagination. Did Kardasha's circumcision really mean anything in the overall scheme of our lives? Absolutely nothing. But it was exciting to play with the idea and be caught up in the event.

On Tuesday, Sekerot, Miton, Sameri, and I drove to our friend's enkang, accompanied by as many supporters as the overloaded, springless Land-Rover would tolerate. As we left camp, Masiene looked at me and asked Sekerot, "Why is he dressed so smartly today?" Unconsciously, I had put on my favorite pair of antique Spanish army fatigues, probably hopeful that the Ololdabash family would not be disappointed in their son's godfather. Before we had passed the invisible boundary designating Ololasurai, two red-ochered Maasai carrying wild olive and pavetta branches to be used for the ceremony at our destination, five miles away, hailed us for a lift. Packed with tent, food, stove, and sleeping bags, the Land-Rover had to be rearranged to make space for these members of my new family. One of the men was Kardasha's handsomely aging uncle, who pulled himself in behind us with two branches the size of Christmas trees.

As tradition defined, instead of bringing his family's cattle in at dusk, Kardasha accompanied them to the corral at noon, after which, on the dung-carpeted floor of the enclosure, he sat amid their lowing. This was the same place where tomorrow he would be circumcised. Next, his head was shaven slick and left gleaming in the harsh midday brilliance. Today his hair dropped to the ground. Tomorrow, at dawn, traces of his body that he would never again touch would be left there.

Later in the afternoon, once the tent had been set under a lone acacia, two hundred yards from the enkang, we returned to the activity in front of the Ololdabash house. Head completely shaved, showing off even to more advantage his striking features, Kardasha moved about the enclosure, the embodiment of grace under pressure, his slim figure now partly shrouded by a loosely fitting, stiff, thin, ash-colored hairless hide. This off-the-shoulder sheath, tied only at the top, left our friend partly bare from the side of his waist downward, to suggest the dress of a Maasai woman, in this case a symbol of fertility. With this simple dull garment against his dusky skin and naked of beaded jewelry, Kardasha's eyes seemed unusually luminous. Today, however, his equally radiant smile was little evident.

Soon bird boys gathered outside the enkang, near the entry of the Ololdabash hut. Each house, which was joined to the next by a wall of circling thorn, had its proper entrance, into which admission was reserved to the corresponding family's cattle. At night, these openings were barricaded with high removable doors constructed of loose sticks and branches. Outside this entryway, Kardasha joined a circle of his age-mates and other youths, who were singing, while in the center of this group one of their number bent his knees slightly to vault straight up into the air, head rising far above the others in soaring leaps. At the pinnacle of his ascent, the dancer not only shimmied his shoulder, but, before returning to earth, shook or lashed his hair like a horse flicking its tail in the breeze. The song that accompanied this display of grace and prowess came from falsetto-voiced soloist. This youth was backed up by a chorus, part of which provided a baritone chant punctuated by the other section's rhythmic guttural sounds which were similar to the dying echoes of a lion's roar.

Inside the enkang, women moved about in preparation. Red-ochered old men, shaded by dung walls, slumped, already drunk with honey-brewed beer or not far from that long-acquainted state of celebration. Kardasha's usually attractive, high-cheeked mother was barely recognizable. She not only appeared to have aged twenty years, but her expression was that of a person overwrought by the news that all family members, distant cousins in-

cluded, had been trampled by a herd of elephants. On the other hand, her husband had taken refuge in honey brew and seemed as absent from the event as when he had visited us days before at Ololasurai. In his usual slow, warm, quiet manner, he could not contain feelings of gratitude, which he repeated again and again and again.

Kardasha's grandmother, like Mary at the foot of the cross, practically fell before us, bestowing every blessing possible upon my person. She now had another son, and a white one at that. Not to be taken lightly were this proud, honest family's expressions of heartfelt gratitude.

We went inside the Ololdabash shelter, which like most Maasai huts was beyond description in its hominess and visual appeal. The suffocating and blinding smoky interior and cockroach-beaded walls hardly distracted from the natural decoration which was enough to elicit admiration from eyes of even the slightest artistic sensitivity.

Upon entering this shelter, one had the feeling, once the eyes stopped watering from the smoke and became acquainted with blackness, of almost complete protection from the elements. The entryway was doorless and stretched a yard before turning sharply left. The far wall of this curve was blocked by a woven reed screen, behind which was a small bedroom for calves, lambs, and kid goats. The angled entryway took the place, in part, of a solid door or curtain. No one could see into the dwelling proper, which was, as well, protected from direct currents of wind. Not being shut off, it also supplied a needed exit for smoke. Once inside the bowels of the structure, anyone six feet or taller was prevented by the ceiling from standing completely upright, except in direct center. Interior walls and roof were faced with a woven screen of termite-resistant branches, tightly laced together with material also stripped from shrubs which termites find unattractive. Onto this lattice, dung was plastered adobe-like to a 203 depth of three to six inches; when dry, it was solid and odorless. The roof was about a foot thick and sturdy to the point of supporting the weight of two or more men, or even six, so Miton told me.

On either side of the living room—kitchen was an alcove berth, one partly walled for seclusion, the other entirely open. These berths varied in size. The first was approximately five feet square, the other slightly smaller. Each was equipped with a small smoke-escape light source, maybe five inches in diameter, midway up the wall. Toward the front of the central room and on the same side as the larger sleeping quarters was another area, partly concealed by a wall with a small open doorway. This six-by-five-foot cubicle, reserved for special use, had recently been converted into Kardasha's berth. Details of house design naturally vary according to the taste of the builder-inhabitants.

In the center of the family room, which measured six by nine feet, was a continuing fire, and above this, in the ceiling, was a hole the size of a tennis ball. Seating in the room was afforded by highly attractive stools, carved from single pieces of wood. The round top of one was almost a foot in diameter, the others smaller. These seats were supported by three legs five to six inches in length. The large single berth in each sleeping quarter was a foot and a half off the ground and fashioned from very stiff stretched hides, slightly rounded on one side to accommodate the outside curve of the domed structure. The berth on the left side of the hut belonged to Kardasha's mother and whoever else she permitted there, her husband included. The sleeping quarter across the room could be shared by anyone. The berths, in shape, did not dictate the sleeping positions of their occupants, who could stretch out in practically any direction, and offered adequate support for five closely sandwiched adults.

Once foreign eyes become acquainted with the smoke and obscurity of the interior, lovely shapes took form, highlighted and shadowed by a slight candle-like kerosene lamp that rested on a solid mantel fashioned of dung. To my eye, the network of woven wall covering and supports against the texture and subtle hue of the solid dung they held offered a far warmer, more naturally simple and pleasing interior, complemented by the functional, unpretentious and sparse Maasai furniture, than did the majority of homes featured in glossy shelter magazines. To the outsider, the question of livability is inevitable, but to Maasai any alternative would be equally unthinkable. Sources of light cast the most wondrous low-key shadows on the persons around us, both moving and static. These pinpointed gleams were made ever changing and enchanting by smoke, and as in other Maasai dwellings, I found them almost hypnotic in appeal. The thick, hard, seemingly porous walls of this house acted as insulation capable of muffling any raised voice, which the inhabitants, I am sure, seldom experienced. I sat on Kardasha's wall-to-wall berth, which was two feet off the ground and had been padded for his soon-to-be sensitive body by a three-inch-thick, hide-covered mattress of fresh olive leaves. Over this would be placed the skin which would be underneath him on the ground tomorrow, the closest witness to the outcome of his ordeal. At the end of the room sat two elders next to leather skins bulging with beer. Into one of these large containers was dipped a slim gourd eight times and the contents divided between the two old men in another important act in the complicated ceremony of circumcision.

Outside, beer flowed in increasing quantities. Dancing and singing became more intense as females chanted while circling and weaving in conga lines. Men and youths covied together, voices joined in strange harmonies, while one of them soared from their midst in leaps of increasing altitude. In the center of this jubilant, speculative crowd, Kardasha appeared strikingly alone, not only set off from the others by his stiff, revealing, dull, armless wrap, but by the look in his eyes, which ranged from detached calm to, now and then, a sideward glance of apprehension, or so it seemed. Once or twice my eyes caught his, or my voice his ear with "Ol chorelai." When he or I was so addressed, the hearer echoed that name in recognition and response. Twice our stares met and a smile relaxed his face, but it was slight and momentary, and most likely nonexistent to other eyes. Only when he paused, out of the crowd, surrounded by cattle, did I sense he might have felt some connection with his surroundings. The animals around him were not marked with the simplified monograms that stamp bovines in America or Spain, nor were their brands restricted to a flank or side. These Maasai bulls, cows, and steers were decorated and identified from the nose to the tail in designs limited only by the imagination of the families and clans to whom they belonged. Equally intriguing were the holes, notches, and splits that perforated the animal's ears to also confirm proof of ownership, and which were far more varied than those cut into Spanish fighting cattle.

Time passed, until my eyes, tracing a dancer's return to earth, focused on the sun brightening a layer of clouds before it slid from cover to sanguine for an instant a horizon plodded by three hundred cattle returning en masse to the enkang. Stretched out in a grand parade a half mile long, they walked solemnly in file while lowing as if to bemoan the day's departure.

L ater that night, when we strolled toward the tent, scores of migrating wildebeest, grunting and croaking, clustered round us. Illuminating them with the torch was like walking through some primeval cave in which stylized prehistoric painted animals stared back at us with mica eyes. As we neared the fire, I wondered how many white men had played godfather for a Maasai's circumcision. Certainly Delamere, probably Finch-Hatton, and in Samburu, Thesiger, for almost certain.

Around the campfire there was endless joking, the subject of which was my suspected nervousness. Examples were given of boys who had winced or even messed themselves under the knife. However, my friends and I were convinced—as much as one could be—that Kardasha would not shame us, his family, and least of all, himself.

At eight o'clock came a moment for which I had been anxious. While the others stayed behind, Sekerot and I, about to witness the inquisition of our friend, walked toward the enkang. During this public hearing, the one to be circumcised must confess any violation of Maasai law. Admission of wrongdoing would not only cast doubt on Kardasha and his family, who were now gathered in the dwelling we were about to enter, but might mean the payment of a cow or goat from a father who had none to spare.

Space had been saved for us—two empty stools—in a room crowded beyond its limit. Even the berths carried as much weight as they could seemingly bear. At our backs was the wall of Kardasha's berth, a foot away its entrance, now partly blocked by the seated Ndorobo circumciser, Ole Kirek, who was about to direct the ceremonial trial that was seconds from commencement. Kardasha and Leperes, a bird boy intimate, sat out of sight on the comfort of the leaf mattress. There was little smoke in a room that 205

now was full of pretrial accusations and suspicions. One man of advanced age was louder that the others, repeating that our friend had once stolen, killed, and eaten the sheep which the accuser had entrusted to his care. When this determined man was stilled—though not for more than the time it took him to draw a breath—other doubts polluted the air.

"What are they saying?" I asked Sekerot.

"There is talk that he has been to bed with a circumcised woman—a cardinal sin," came the whispered reply.

"What do you think?" I asked, seeking reassurance that our friend was pure except for lovemaking with uncut girls.

"Well," frowned Sekerot, "clouds usually indicate rain."

Oh, how Walt Disney would have offered a lifetime film contract to the Ndorobo, Ole Kirek, who was about to call the trial to order. Thank goodness, he never appeared in those feature cartoons that flickered the screen of the Alex Theatre, where, during a projection of *Pinocchio*, as the whale swallowed everything in sight, my father, swayed by the pleas of his five-year-old twins, took our trembling hands and led us into the popcorn smells, soft orange light, and security of the lobby.

As we half turned to face the bedroom door, Sekerot's dim torch reflected the glints and gleams of the Ndorobo's eyes and the sly smile of a man whose conscience seemed to know few boundaries. It was almost as if we had privileged seats next to the devil himself. Beside Ole Kirek squatted his associate, who was an equally nasty little piece of work. Now that our eyes had adjusted more to the available light, we could see the gallery of etched, creased, and cracked faces become immobile in anticipation.

Would the boy on trial, loved and admired by many of them, be found tainted or judged pure?

This cast of sages, evil sorcerer, determined accuser, honorable questioner, overwrought mother, handsome young hero out to prove pre-warrior innocence, his loyal friends, and the dark beauties waiting outside under the stars is what grand opera is all about. If Puccini had once stumbled onto such a scene, one could be sure here would have been the inspiration for Act V of *Turandot*.

The Ndorobo took charge. First called was Kardasha, out of sight, who crawled forward on the mattress so that his face was visible. Then, to the accompaniment of special words, the Ndorobo pulled a slim gourd from beneath his garment and, removing the lid, dipped a thumb into the white lime it contained. The thumb was then slowly drawn four times from the bridge between our friend's eyes to the tip of his nose, leaving a strip of white to mark him protagonist of the now opened trial. Since I was unwilling to have a single world escape memory or be left to misinterpretation, a micro tape recorder was switched on in Sekerot's hand, igniting an almost undetectable red light that pulsated not only with every accusing word, but with the answers of Kardasha, who again sat out of sight in the room behind us.

NDOROBO: "Be quiet, everyone!"

OLD MAN: "Give that boy a place to pass. Let Kardasha come to the front of the bed."

PEOPLE IN THE CROWD: "Let the boy pass. Let him pass."

NDOROBO (to Kardasha): "My little warrior, is it not true that what is about to happen here, as well as what will happen tomorrow morning, will be of importance not only in the future of your mother, your father, of me, Ole Kirek, as well as of the man who will support your back tomorrow, Ole Pirianoi? Actually, the outcome of these events will affect almost everyone in this room. Is it not for this reason that we are gathered here? So, I'm telling you to openly confess five sins that I know you have committed. [Guilty until proven innocent.] Now, I am going to ask you those five questions. If you are guilty of these acts, it is your option to cover them with lies if you have to, but then you will be responsible for the punishment and curses that will not only fall upon you, but upon everyone in this room.

"First, do you have only one testicle? Second, did your mother give birth to you before she was circumcised? Third, since children fight when they are young, have you ever lost control and broken a bone of a playmate or caused serious injury to anyone? Fourth, now about women. These days we know that young and old men indiscriminately sleep with anyone. There are so many loose women drunks around. Even your father, or any man who wants, can go with them. So, the question is, have you slept with a circumcised woman? Fifth, have you ever used tobacco, which your father should never have allowed until you were circumcised? When you have answered these questions, anyone else with grievances or evidence against you may ask whatever he wishes. Now, answer those five questions."

[Fines for having committed the above mentioned crimes are: 1)for having one testicle, the payment of a cow to the Ndorobo, 2) for having been born of an uncircumcised woman, the payment of one cow, 3) for having injured another person, the payment of a cow or steer to the wounded one, 4) for having slept with a circumcised woman, the payment by the boy of one cow to his family and another to the circumciser, and 5) for having used tobacco, the payment of a cow to his father.]

THE CROWD: "Now it's time for the boy to talk. Let him speak."

OLD MAN: "Kardasha, tell the truth about those five things. If you don't you may die."

THE CROWD: "Let him answer those questions about matters which guide our world."

KARDASHA: "I have two testicles. I have not slept with a circumcised woman. I've never broken the bone of any child. And I don't know if my mother gave birth to me when she was uncircumcised because I never asked her. Also, I've never used tobacco."

NDOROBO: "Your father knows whether you have lied or not about all these sins but one. There is one thing about which no one knows the truth but you. Only you can answer this question. Now, I offer you the chance to confess if you have just lied. Reconsider. Have you or have you not slept with a circumcised woman? Your father doesn't know if you have. I don't know. You are the only person in this room who can answer that question."

THE CROWD: "You Kirek, be quiet. You heard his answer. We know he's not guilty of that!"

NDOROBO: "Now, I say, if you have committed these sins and you've lied to me, Ole Kirek, and you've lied to Ole Pirianoi, and you've lied to your mother and to every single person in this house, may the truth seek its revenge and punish you. May my knife slip tomorrow and cut more than its obligation, causing you pain and illness." [The object of tomorrow's surgery, the penis, is being threatened with amputation.]

THE CROWD: "May God listen!"

NDOROBO: "I'm putting you on a spot, from which

there is no return. If you lie, may tomorrow bring wrath upon you. When your legs are opened like a woman's and I sit between them, may the cut of my knife burn you with pain. If you have not committed these sins, may life be good to you."

THE CROWD: "May God listen and bless you!"

NDOROBO: "May you succeed in everything you do."

THE CROWD: "May God listen and bless you!"

NDOROBO: "May your scar bring you many cattle."

THE CROWD: "May God listen and bless you!"

NDOROBO: "May your scar bring you many wives."

THE CROWD: "May God listen and bless you!"

NDOROBO: "May your scar bring you many children."

THE CROWD: "May God listen and bless you!"

NDOROBO: "Let's all join together and wish that your children may prosper."

THE CROWD: "May God listen and bless you!"

OLE PIRIANOI: "Now, everyone be still because my question is the only one that remains. Later we will deal with the theft. Tell those men to be quiet. I'm not going to ask the boy if his mother gave birth to him before she was circumcised because I've always known the family, and I can verify that she bore him after she had been cut. [Turning to Kardasha] Neither am I going to ask if you have one testicle because I have seen with my own eyes that you have two. Neither am I going to ask if you have wounded another child or used tobacco, for I know that you haven't. Are these not the four things that I won't ask? I have one, and only one, question. Have you slept with an uncircumcised woman? I've know this boy since he was an infant, and that's how I'm aware he's not guilty of the other sins. About this sin, I am not sure because it is impossible for me to follow him everywhere. I don't know where he's slept, and with whom. His mother doesn't

know. His father doesn't know. And none of you in this house knows. Remember [Kardasha] tomorrow it is I who will be supporting you as you lean on me. I can't understand why you are hiding this one thing from us. Speak up and confess, because if you lied, your father and mother, as well as I, will fall in disgrace. You will curse us with bad luck. If you lie, may you be greatly harmed."

THE CROWD: "May God let it happen. May he be cursed and harmed!"

NDOROBO: "Yes. May God listen."

THE CROWD: "You are right. May God punish if punishment is deserved!"

OLE PIRIANOI: "And if it's true that you did not commit this sin, may the knife be cold tomorrow and cause you no pain."

THE CROWD: "May God bless you!"

OLE PIRIANOI: "May the arrow that is shot into the bull cleanly pierce the vein to provide you with blood."

THE CROWD: "May God listen!"

OLE PIRIANOI: "May food be of benefit to you when you eat."

THE CROWD: "May God listen!"

OLE PIRIANOI: "May the guests not vomit the food that is offered them at the celebration."

THE CROWD: "Let God hear you!"

OLE PIRIANOI: "May they not vomit the food that your white father has provided."

THE CROWD: "May God listen!"

OLE PIRIANOI: "May Ole Kirek also benefit from the food and may it guide his hand to help when he cuts to spill your blood."

THE CROWD: "May God listen!"

OLE PIRIANOI: "May your wound heal fast."

THE CROWD: "May God bless you!"

OLE PIRIANOI: "May you not throw up the blood."

THE CROWD: "May God bless you!"

OLE PIRIANOI: "May you not vomit the oil."

THE CROWD: "May God listen!"

OLE PIRIANOI: "May you not vomit the milk and blood!"

THE CROWD: "May God listen!"

OLE PIRIANOI: "May all blessings and good things come to you."

THE CROWD: "Let God hear that!"

OLE PIRIANOI: "May your fame roll like thunder to be heard far, and cause you to become a great leader."

THE CROWD: "May God listen!"

OLE PIRIANOI: "May you enjoy a long life and grow to old age."

A MEMBER OF THE CROWD: "What about the theft the boy committed?"

NDOROBO: "All right. Everyone quiet now."

THE CROWD: "Tell the white godfather what is happening. Tell him what this is all about."

NDOROBO: "The boy has denied everything, hasn't he? If the boy is pure, I will receive the one goat owed. If he is not, then he will pay with pain or death."

FATHER OF KARDASHA: "My son, tell them you haven't stolen anything."

SHEEP OWNER: "All right. You. [Kardasha] Step forth and tell me about my bronze-colored sheep. Come now and tell me what you did with that sheep, because tomorrow's blade belongs to me as much as to the Ndorobo. Every person in this room will be circumcising you tomorrow. Don't kid yourself. We also wield the knife."

ONE MAN: "Put a curse on the boy! Curse him!"

THE CROWD: "Let's find out about the sheep. [To the owner] Don't let him get by without learning what happened to your sheep. That sheep was there, and then it was gone. Kardasha, tell us right now if you took it."

SHEEP OWNER: "My little grandfather [pet name this man used for Kardasha], we know you didn't eat the lamb because Maasai are not permitted to eat baby animals. But is it not possible that your herding stick unconsciously led it astray? Doesn't a herding staff occasionally stray and an animal get lost? Say, for instance, I go and herd sheep. Isn't it possible for my stick to go astray and a sheep could be left behind in the bush? Or are you saying that a stick from the Ololdabash family never goes astray?"

KARDASHA: "Yes, it is possible for my stick to go astray. But that day it did not!"

SHEEP OWNER: "That day how could a young sheep leave the rest by itself and get lost! You know that morning I put three lambs in your care, and you only returned with two."

THE CROWD: "Then curse him! Curse him right now!"

KARDASHA'S COUSIN (to Kardasha): "Don't fear, because if you committed the theft, it will be my responsibility to compensate this man, even if he wants a sheep, a calf, or a heifer. Don't worry. I'll give him anything he wishes. Don't be afraid to tell the truth. Don't lie. I'll provide anything he desires, even money. I'm not going to ask anyone to help me pay this debt, and all of you men are witness to my words and commitment."

THE CROWD (to sheep owner): "Go ahead and curse him, for if he insists he didn't steal the lamb, the only way we'll ever know if he's guilty is when he screams under tomorrow's knife."

KARDASHA'S FATHER: "Go ahead and curse my son."

OLD MAN (to sheep owner): "Go ahead and curse him,

unless you don't know how to put a curse on someone."

ANOTHER MAN: "All of you, shut up, and let the sheep's owner get to the bottom of this. Let him handle his own case. Stop interfering with your curses to distract from the real issue at point."

SHEEP OWNER: "It's these relatives of Kardasha's who were also making noise last night because they were drinking too much beer. Kardasha, don't I have cattle that I would willingly offer so that an arrow can pierce a vein to provide you with blood for tomorrow's ceremony? Do you believe I can let you think I wish to curse you only so that you will bleed to death under the Ndorobo's knife in the morning? But, all the same, remember, we all know of a boy who refused to tell the truth about a stolen animal, and he died under the circumciser's blade. Don't be deaf to my words. Now, tell me about the stick that went astray. Why wait? Why draw this out? You know that as long as I live I'll keep hounding you about this until you confess. I'll never tire of asking."

SOME MEMBERS OF THE CROWD: "Curse him!"

OTHER MEMBERS OF THE CROWD: "Bless him!"

SHEEP OWNER: "The hide you will sit on tomorrow has always been used for circumcisions in this enkang. It was used for your older brother. It can tell a boy who lies from one who tells the truth. Now it is your turn. Do you think you can escape unharmed? The morning will give the answer. The morning will tell if you've lied. But if you really did not steal the sheep, may that lost lamb help you! [he shouts] If you are pure, don't let these accusations panic you!"

THE CROWD: "You've already said that. Everything has been said."

SHEEP OWNER: "My age group supports you. You have

been put under our protective wings. And if you did steal my sheep, let the morning be the judge!"

THE CROWD: "*Kijape* [sheep owner], let's end all of this now. Enough has been said."

SHEEP OWNER: "Then bless the boy!"

THE CROWD: "May God listen to your blessings for Kardasha."

With the trial finished, the crowd started drinking and singing songs they had sung as warriors. Following are fragments of songs sung by soloist and chorus after Kardasha's trial:

"Oh, great god, Engai, whom we praise, who doesn't eat the impurities that uncircumcised boys eat."

"Oh, my sweet cow. May your name inspire us to be brave and never drop our shields in retreat."

"May the seed of the cow that came from our raided enemies prosper. When our steers pass through the thornbushes, may they be protected from the white Egyptian vultures."

"Listen to how we spear elephants who are enormous as caverns. We speared the elephant behind the shoulder and in the neck. And we met lions sleeping and awoke them with the kudu horn. I blew the horn only once; then the lion came to me. When the lion came to me, it infested me with the flies that crazed it. Then I speared it straight through the cheek to cool its rage. Let's show this proud lioness the kind of fight she's looking for. . . ."

The trial was over and we returned to the tent. While my young Maasai friends circled the campfire exchanging words sung and spoken, I crawled into the sleeping bag, knowing that I would have to be out of it before six the next morning. I thought the deep croaking of wildebeest, like foghorns in the night, would lull me to sleep. But from ten o'clock until two in the morning anxious dreams relentlessly disturbed a half slumber. In one of these semiconscious excursions, Sekerot and I sat in a room jostled and racked by an earthquake of the gravest magnitude, and while I attempted to convince him of its seriousness, he totally ignored the happening. Later, we were in Lisbon, staring from a hotel window while a flood of brown water swept the street below clear of everything in sight, people and cars included. These nightmares grew in intensity and distastefulness until I came awake to the croaking of wildebeest, which, not more than twenty feet away, had circled the tent.

With a roll of toilet paper in hand, I unzipped the mosquito netting and walked only as far as my conscience demanded (some thirty yards). Here, there was no question of locating one place better than the other to squat, for the ground stretched bare and flat in all directions. Before leaving the tent, I had been unable to find a torch. Now, in this vulnerable position, with the tent distant enough in ground fog to be barely discernible, I thought of our Ololasurai outhouse and was thankful that it was minimally enclosed by a back wall and two sides, though the front was open. Here on the plain, protection seemed to rest only with the wildebeest that surrounded me, heads up, concerned not only with my presence at this hour, but possibly more so with my attitude. If a lion was on the prowl, I felt some assurance that antelope alarms would betray its proximity.

In the distance, rising out of the mist, was a jagged thicket of thorn where three days ago cattle guided by Kardasha had stampeded away from lions hidden there. Sekerot was sure that this was the same pride of four females and an immature male that once, when he had stopped near the Ololdabash enkang, had slunk low, crouching while stalking him and his car. Of more concern was the report he had brought back from Sekenani Camp, told to him by our French friend Jean Marie Sabin, who two nights ago had been driving through heavy rain toward the Mara. It had been late and, with the storm making him anxious to reach Sekenani, Jean Marie had pushed on with as much speed as the road would permit. He knew the pitted route practically by memory, but the rain obscured a curve, which spun him directly into a group of five lions stretched out in the path. Attempting to avoid the animals, Jean Marie steered the car off the road and into a ditch, where it was immediately pounced upon by the largest of the lionesses and by an immature male. The driver's window was down, and through this the lioness slid a paw, attempting to sink her claws into our French friend, who grabbed a torch and, with it, struck his attacker, at the same time blinding her with the beam. In this way, he was able to hold off the lioness's repeated charges. Meanwhile, the immature male, standing on hind legs, scratched with forepaw claws at the passenger-side window glass, which, with little effort, he could have smashed.

Finally, Jean Marie was able to start the car and sputter out of the ditch to continue eight hundred yards down the road, where the engine again died. As the rain fell harder, Jean Marie got out of the car with the hope of tightening a loose sparkplug, only to hear the lions pounding down the wet road toward him in a new attack. Back in the car, he was able to start the engine and jerk away as the lions tore with their claws at the vehicle's rear bumper. Jean Marie's encounter with the lions had taken place two days before and five hundred yards from where I now squatted.

Once back in the tent, I relinquished thoughts of sleep and gave in to the merry-go-round of bizarre images circling in my mind. At the center of this whirl was the moment of truth which first light would summon.

Torchless and having pressed with a fingernail the mode button on my watch instead of one that would light it, again I unzipped the tent. Beyond the facing mountains, sky showed only the faintest pale. Eyes that had squinted too many years into camera viewfinders or at thousands of transparencies had not the least chance of reading the digital numbers and hour on the watch. I crept inside the tent and awakened Sekerot. It was five-thirty. By the time we had dressed and prepared ourselves with everything needed to record the morning's happening, it was six-fifteen.

Outside the still closed gateway to the Ololdabash side of the corral, we waited in the dim light until Papore Ole Kool appeared, followed by his cousin Kardasha, bird boys, and a half dozen other youths. The gate was removed to release the day's protagonist and his entourage, which now joined us, though as we moved forward toward a stream a hundred yards distant, the bird boys fell behind and waited. Once at the water, Kardasha, following his cousin's instructions, removed the leather sheath and, in the morning chill, splashed his nakedness until it was rimmed white gold, glistening subtly in the dawn. Beyond him, acacias and wildebeest stood like black figures cut from paper against the grayness of the landscape.

Kardasha, the stress of the moment now boldly scrawled across his face—or was it merely the chill?—again covered his body and led us toward the enkang. Receiving our approach was the charcoal-figured band of bird boys rattling fine sticks in increasing rhythm while chanting, after which one of this fraternity met the rising sun and Kardasha with shouted song. As the sun tried to glimmer through a slight crack which separated stratum after stratum of clouds from mountains on the horizon, this somber, but animated, procession neared the thorn fence with intensifying chants, beating of sticks, and songs.

BIRD BOY SOLOIST: "All of you uncircumcised boys show nothing but bad manners, especially to your mothers and fathers." [Blasphemy in Maasai society.]

CHORUS: "Oeoyioeoeo yoo-oyia."

BIRD BOY SOLOIST: "You're so negligent that you allow the gray bull, the prize sire of the herds, to stray and become covered with flies."

CHORUS: "Oeoyioeoeo yoo-oyia."

BIRD BOY SOLOIST: "And oh, all of you boys who fear the knife have gluttonous mothers with swollen bellies. And do you know why they are that way? Because they drink the blood of cowards. They also eat slimy, stinky residue from foreskins, as well as collect all covered penises like yours, from enkang to enkang, until no one can stand the stench."

CHORUS: "Oeoyioeoeo yoo-oyia."

[The obvious purpose of these words was to cause Kardasha to rebel and be even more repulsed by his uncircumcised body, to desire nothing more than to be made clean and a man by the Ndorobo's waiting knife.]

BIRD BOY SOLOIST: "An uncircumcised boy does not make a good man, and he'll never have a good neighbor. He's a person who can't solve his own problems. He's a scavenger who slinks around. He's a dirty cur, good for nothing but collecting discarded bones."

CHORUS: "Oeoyioeoeo yoo-oyia."

BIRD BOY SOLOIST: "You slither about the house at night, you filthy beggar, and in the darkness abuse innocent women while they slumber."

CHORUS: "Oeoyioeoeo yoo-oyia."

Once through the thorn wall and onto the soft dung floor of the enkang proper, activity accelerated as the atmosphere tensed beyond any limits I had before experienced. Only the running of the bulls in Pamplona, where men and beasts enter the ring tunnel and burst out onto the sand, had any similarity in my frame of reference to the tenseness of this event. Song, shouts, screams, and beating of sticks crescendoed. Faces, beads, and tunics blurred together as the sheath of leather was removed and Kardasha stood naked, exposing a body that would undergo change as would, of more importance, his person. Women, not allowed to watch the operation, suddenly disappeared.

Now produced was a ceramic pot, which the night before had been filled with cold water and into which had been placed a small metal hide scraper to increase the chill. The liquid content of this vessel was poured over Kardasha's cleanly shaved head. The effect of the icy

water, Miton had told me, combined with the morning cold, is just enough to jolt the already psyched-out mind and body into a semi-conscious state of shock. Ole Pirianoi, the holder, now stood behind Kardasha and, with his arms, circled our friend's chest. At this instant, Kardasha's body collapsed as if in a faint, eyes shut, chin resting on chest, limbs flaccid, and he was half carried, his heels furrowing the dung, to the special hide that now stretched the ground. This skin had been positioned between two planted branches selected from a ceremonial tree.

The Ndorobo surgeon, Ole Kirek, squatting between Kardasha's spread legs, dipped his thumb into a slim gourd of lime and marked our friend's nose with a white line. The frenzied bird boys chanted threats fused with encouragement, which would continue through the operation, building in rapidity and volume, while elders, preparing for the worst, cast doubt on Kardasha's bravery.

BIRD BOYS: "Lie as still as if you were dead! That's it! You're dead! You're dead! Dead ones feel nothing! As yet, you haven't given us reason to despise you. Don't do it! Keep dying! Don't let the Ndorobo make you flinch. Don't show you feel his knife. You can't run from it. You're dead! The dead feel no pain! Die, you beggar! Die!"

The Ndorobo was now fingering and peeling back Kardasha's foreskin. This operation could be divided into five steps: 1) The foreskin was peeled back from the penis head and the cord attached to its underside was cut. 2) Now completely free of the penis head, the foreskin was rolled back further, like a sock down an ankle, and spread by the circumciser's fingers, while the knife, an inch and a half back from where the foreskin joined the penis shaft, began cutting, circling the foreskin, slicing delicately to divide the single sheet of flesh into two parts, which, when pulled forward, separated from one another like a gummed label from a piece of paper. 3) Once the foreskin had been separated, it was stretched forward over the penis head. The sheath was now double the length of its unoperated-on state. 4) Next, the Ndorobo cut a hole midway along and in the top of the extended foreskin. Through this opening the penis head was pulled, the foreskin now fitting between the head and the shaft, like a necktie pulled tightly around a man's throat. The excess foreskin dangled from below the head. 5) Now the hanging rough rectangle of foreskin was taken in the Ndorobo's fingers and, with seemingly excessive cutting, pared and shaped so that it hung, fashioned into a point. This was a highly critical part of the operation and was of almost as much concern to the patient, surgeon, and everyone else involved as would be a cosmetic surgery job done on an aging movie star—it was something that would be admired or criticized for the remainder of a lifetime. Of equal importance, a long and well-shaped tie is thought to give a decided advantage in lovemaking, both for the stimulation it provokes and the response it elicits.

BIRD BOYS: "Die! Die! Die! It's almost over!"

THE CROWD: "Ole Kirek, don't make his tie too short! Don't spoil it. Take your time! Do a good job!"

Kardasha's face communicated, if you can call it that, absolute absence. The contrast between pain felt at its zenith and the beauty of total concentration and control was enough to take one's breath away. Accompanied by wave after pounding wave of chanted encouragement, our friend lay as one might have observed him had he rested

on a state-of-the-art operating table in New York, Paris, or London, fogged out of conscious expression by a massive dose of sodium pentothal. Michelangelo would have smashed the *Pietà* to bits and begun anew had he chanced upon the glistening boy before us, half-fallen head, expression somewhere between far-off concentration and sleep, muscled shoulders, arms, chest, abdomen, and thighs ignited by the sun's filtered rays. From the instant Ole Kirek's knife made the first white incision until it sliced its last cut, Kardasha's body had been as immobile as if it had been cast in bronze.

AN OLD MAN: "All of you keep quiet, because this is almost over!"

KARDASHA'S UNCLE TO A WOMAN: "Bring that cow! Milk the sacred cow! Take the sheep to the doorway!"

KARDASHA'S COUSIN TO A SOBBING BOY: "Stop crying. Don't you see he didn't move? He was like a stone. You've nothing to be ashamed of. Don't you see?"

THE CROWD: "Bring the milk! The Ndorobo had done a good job."

NDOROBO (to the bird boys): "Do you see anything wrong with this circumcision? Do you have any questions?"

BIRD BOYS: "Aren't we able to see for ourselves? Just pour the milk so we can carry him into the house."

[The Ndorobo poured milk over Kardasha's bloodied loins, after which our friend, still limp in trance, was raised by the holder, Ole Pirianoi.]

KARDASHA'S UNCLE: "Doesn't this boy have shoes? Bring the initiate's shoes." [Sandals of thin leather are specially made for the newly circumcised boy.]

KARDASHA'S COUSIN: "You boys, help the holder with him."

BIRD BOY: "Hold his back and I'll take his legs."

BIRD BOY (to Kardasha): "Don't speak a word until you've drunk the blood inside."

BIRD BOY (to Kardasha): "Keep your penis tie away from the hide on your bed."

BIRD BOY: "Tell his white father that no one can speak to him until he's taken the blood."

Now, amid praising voices and great sighs of relief, the bird boys grabbed the arms and legs of their friend, bloodied from his birth into manhood, and carried him, still flaccid, like Christ from the cross, toward the darkness of his mother's hut. As the doorway was passed, a lamb, held across its threshold was splattered with blood of the Maasai who never again would greet any man with a bowed head, but with the shake of a hand.

By the time we arrived at the doorway, the lamb was being slaughtered on the floor where it lay, its blood mixing with that of Kardasha. "How brave. How brave," came the voices. "He didn't move a finger. Not an eyelash. He proved he was even stronger than we suspected. Congratulations, Ol ashumpai. You have a brave son." The pride I felt was subservient to my happiness for this gentle, strong, kind boy and for the family who loved their son, brother, nephew, cousin, and grandson, and who now moved about, returning to the enkang from varying states of shock and fear to bask in a glory which, after all, was their own.

When we were at last able to push through the gawkers and well-wishers, I sat on the edge of Kardasha's bed, as so many times in the past I had sat next to Spanish gladiators who had succeeded against all odds in Iberian or Mexican *plazas de toros*. Bandaged and bloodied legs or arms were little to pay in pain for the moments of glory that had preceded and followed. Of more hurt than a wounded body would have been the suffering and the condemning silence that comes from a show of cowardice.

Kardasha's drawn lids concealed the brightness of his eyes as his right hand held blood and flesh that would before long know as many lovers as his endurance could entertain. In the slight light, his profile was barely visible, as his eyes remained closed. "Let us go out and see the blood drawn," whispered Sekerot. "Anyway, you cannot speak with him until he has drunk it." Before we departed, a clip of hair from the white sacred cow was tied by a woman to the neck string of Kardasha's cloak. I was told that this would help ward off "the little biting teeth," as pain from the circumcision wound is known.

In the corral, two boys held a white steer calf, while a tourniquet was tightened around its lower neck to bulge the jugular vein. When enough blood had been trapped, a youth arrived with bow and arrow, which had been dulled so that it would pierce only the skin and vein. While the calf was held, each time with more difficulty, this Maasai archer attempted twice without success to pierce the white hide. Either the skin was too tough or the vein not prominent enough, so the calf was released and a larger one selected. This white, immature bullock was one of the most strikingly handsome animals in the corral. Anyone with an eye for cattle would have been taken with his good looks. Again the archer tried, and failed twice. The crowd was growing impatient. Kardasha waited in the hut, unable to speak to anyone before he drank milk just squeezed from the white, sacred cow mixed with the fresh blood that waited to be drawn from the bullock in front of us.

Finally, Papore, our friend's cousin, snatched the bow, and in a second had pierced the vein. The spurt of blood was gathered in a slim calabash by a girl of dark, delicate beauty. A patch of damp dung was then pressed against the bullock's neck to stop bleeding.

We accompanied this drink as it was taken hot and uncoagulated into the hut's darkness, where it was poured into another calabash which contained milk from the white cow. Milk from this sacred animal had already glistened Kardasha's loins, and she had as well provided the hair that twisted around his neck strap. At a distance across the room from which he was visible to us, but not we to him, we watched Kardasha, eyes now opened, as a woman tried to offer him the calabash of blood and milk.

"Don't take any blood until you have been given cows," whispered Leperes, his bird boy intimate, who had often visited the tent at Ololasurai. When a youth has shown courage under the knife, family and friends reward his exemplary behavior with material expressions of gratitude: sheep, goats, and cows.

OLD WOMAN: "Somebody give this boy a cow, because until that's done, he won't drink from the calabash, which will grow cold and the blood will clot."

KARDASHA'S MOTHER: "Take the blood and I'll give you the black heifer, the daughter of Enkiteng."

A YOUNG BOY: "Take the blood and I'll give you that little brown sheep."

KARDASHA'S COUSIN: "I give you two goats. Now you can take the blood."

Kardasha had not shown such bravery to have it so little rewarded. He did not speak, but stared expressionless at the calabash. Then I moved forward and sat on the bed. Sekerot interpreted, as only he could do, as fast as the words fell from my lips, faithful in meaning as well as nuance. "That blood is from one of the most handsome bullocks I have ever seen," I said. "When you drink it, he will be part of you, and since you possess his blood, he should be yours, as well. I offer him to you, and that is little reward for the bravery you have shown." Kardasha took the calabash, closed his eyes, and swallowed gulp after gulp, not moving his lips from the mouth of the gourd until it was empty. "Ol chorelai," he softly said,

extending his bloody hand, which could at last accept mine. This was not the usual Maasai, man-to-man, loose, rapid, barely-there-at-all greeting in which palms often slightly make contact with one another. For several seconds the boy's hand tightly gripped my own, as his sensitivity and insight provoked him into a show of affection in which he realized that, while Maasai through and through, he was now also dealing with another world of expression.

Outside, guests continued to arrive. They came from the great expanses of flatness that surrounded the enkang. Distant figures, barely visible, appeared alone or in numbers, all drawn in the same direction. The delicacy of this scene defied words. It could not have successfully been represented by a still camera, and barely in a painting.

Women came in files like brilliant spokes leading to the hub of the enkang. They were not only ochered but wore their finest tinkling head ornaments, and beaded collar after collar of the most vivid mixed colors: red, white, blue, and orange predominating. Indistinguishable female voices came and went with the whims of the breeze. But, drawing closer, we heard clear chorused songs which announced the joy of this day. For some of them, the boy they celebrated might soon be lover and one day a husband.

Old men came singly or in pairs, red figures that seemed the only points of color in the enormity of the surrounding pastel. As they slowly neared, walking sticks took form, as did the bold-woven patterns of blankets that draped their shoulders, fluttering, like trains of exotic birds, above the ocher stubble.

However, what was most moving in this oncoming flow of well-wishers were not the colorful groups of beaded, seductive girls or bright-blanketed elders, but the processions of somber, tunicked bird boys, their feathered headdresses swaying and rising like jagged halos against the midday brightness. Beyond these future warriors, also muted in tones of charcoal, migrating wildebeest paraded endlessly from one extreme of the horizon to the other. Suddenly, I experienced a glow that persisted within my being and without. Was Kardasha's celebration cause for this rare state? Not entirely. I think the glow was simply and merely at last feeling a part of Africa, of fitting that piece of myself into the one empty space in the puzzle of my existence.

Before we abandoned the corral, ready to return to the tent for breakfast, we were stopped by the old man who last night had so assuredly accused Kardasha of thievery. "That boy is clean beyond doubt," he said to Sekerot. "Tell him," he pointed to me, "that boy is innocent beyond reproach. The knife cut the way for truth." The old man's emotion-laden words were another example of the Maasai way, in which forgiveness or acceptance comes willingly in the face of a seemingly proven mistake.

The circumcision over, it was time for "Dr. Kirek," as we called the Ndorobo, to collect his fee, which he chose to have in cash instead of in the flesh of a sheep. While the circumciser had earlier demanded payment (which he had been denied) in exchange for being photographed, he now posed willingly. When the session was finished, he still postured, not satisfied with my ability to record his every mood. And in this, he was absolutely correct. Even if we were joined by Avedon, Douglas-Duncan, and Penn, as well as Stieglitz and Adams brought back for the occasion, one or two of the Ndorobo's countless expressions would still have escaped impression on film. Kirek and his assistant, squatting against a dung wall, counting and re-

counting the bills, each time with increasing satisfaction and smiles, could have just as easily been in a rear office of New York's garment district, rejoicing at a deal well made.

We were back and forth from the tent to singing and dancing in the enkang, where beer and people flowed without hesitation. Several elders produced a bottle of clear liquid, which must have been nearly pure alcohol, for, seconds after consumption, the veins on their shaved heads seemed to double. However jubilant the crowd, one serious part of the circumcision ceremony had been left undone, the result of which could be far more painful to Kardasha than the cuts that had already wounded his body.

Sometime after midday, when Sekerot and friends had strolled back to the enkang, I stayed in camp and stretched out on the ground, listening to wind whistling through the thatch of the umbrella acacia. While in its shade I was joined by a quartet of week-old calves which slept, then rose to stretch themselves or rub heads before settling in puffs of dust back to the warm ground. With them, I felt in harmony as, before us, the celebration continued unshielded from the sun.

In the distance, the muted, flat enkang seemed changed from the way it had appeared yesterday. First, two wild olive boughs had been planted straight up on either side of Kardasha's house to designate it as the home of a new man, who would begin a new life. These delicate green banners were not all that rose above the wall of thorn. There was song, and with it appeared dancers, propelled not only by strong legs, but by the exuberance of the occasion, small figures rising above the hut roofs to join the far-off flat tops of acacias that broke the horizon.

At three in the afternoon, Kardasha, emerging from the darkness of the hut and the shock of his ordeal, blinked into the harsh sunlight, which now lit the man who hours before had been a boy. Escorted by the Ndorobo to outside the family gate, he again sat on the ground, surrounded by age-mates and elders, while Ole Kirek's slender fingers once more touched the bloody foreskin, this time for inspection, hopeful of approval. If the swollen, hemorrhaged skin had been improperly or unartistically sliced, the circumcision would be repeated and corrected. This does occur, as Sekerot's cousin whispered to me—it had happened to him. If the first circumcision had been barely tolerable, the second, he told me, was of a pain more hideous than anyone but the victim can imagine.

For five minutes, Kardasha was not only openly scrutinized by the Ndorobo, but by everyone else around. That one's sex is publicly displayed is no shame, but a pride in which the last signs of childhood are now shown to have been cut away. Had sufficient skin been sliced? Had too much been removed? Had the dangling tie been neatly, evenly fashioned? Or did it need more paring? Did it terminate in a well-shaped point? The agonizing thought of an encore was almost too much to bear.

Kirek fingered and displayed his handiwork for my inspection, smiling smugly with the security of a job artfully completed. As Kardasha slowly got to his feet, he grinned at us before taking the steps that led to refuge, newly experienced pampering and darkness, where he would at last begin fashioning into a headdress the birds that had taken a year to collect. He would not leave the smoky dimness of home and the comfort of his leaf-stuffed mattress for two days, during which time, under subsiding pain, he would take the greatest care not to allow his swollen penis tie to touch the hardness of the skin hide that had been witness to his sudden entry into manhood. Miton told me that he, uninformed about the dangers of contact between the two skins, one his own, the other the hide under him, had let them touch. With the infection that followed, half of the dangling tie brittled and dropped from his body. A long tie, as well as supposedly giving more pleasure to a girl during lovemaking, is also thought to ward off venereal disease. So, its importance to a Maasai youth like Kardasha, soon free to conquer all females around him, could not be underestimated. As we prepared to break camp and depart, my friend's father made me the gift of a very round black and white nanny goat.

Several days later, when we again visited the Ololdabash enkang and Kardasha at his bedside, he seemed drawn and detached. Could anyone expect him to be otherwise? We spoke of his bravery and of his plans for warriorhood, assuring him that my role had not ended with circumcision. From his new relation he would immediately count on a black cloth for a bird boy shuka, and a goat when one was needed to be killed to provide special ceremonial oil with which to annoint his body. Unlike his friend, Leperes, who had already passed six months as a bird boy, Kardasha's feathered headdress would know far less wind. In five months time, when Leperes's head would be reshaved to free him of the intermediate bird boy status and its restrictions, Kardasha would join him so that, together, they could proceed into warriorhood. A youth cannot enter into warriorhood alone. The basic rule that a moran must eat in the company of another warrior would in itself make solo entry an impossibility. When the

time came for Kardasha to cast away his bird boy halo it would be left to me to again honor him, this time with a spear and ocher. In my absence, Sekerot would attend to his needs. As we prepared to depart, Kardasha rose from the bed, put on his headdress of forty-eight bird skins, and said he would accompany us to outside the enkang's wall of thorn. As we walked, he and I before the others, he took my hand in his and twined his fingers among mine. In almost any other part of the world, persons seeing us would have read sexuality into that contact. In Maasailand it was no more meaningful than a simple smile shared between two friends. The younger could have been daydreaming of a quietly beautiful girl from the next enkang, while the older one was thinking of the little time that remained to find Cape buffalo.

Returning to camp from Kardasha's circumcision was like going home after a weekend away that seemed more like an absence of several months. Once at Ololasurai, Sekerot and Miton hastily repacked and climbed back into the Land-Rover which would carry them to the nearest town, Narok. I was left in camp with Sameri, Sekerot's delightful twelve-year-old reed of a brother, as well as with Masiene and Moseka.

Once my friends had left, I reflected on Kardasha's circumcision. Short weeks ago, I had come to Africa burnt out by certain events in my life. Journeying to Kenya I had connected with the healing force of Nature. In Ololasurai itself I had found a passionate love and had, if you will, thrown myself into its bed, forgetting any of the many risks that this involved. I had come to Africa to escape human problems, to be intensely involved with Nature in its most powerful manifestation. Yet ironically, through a chance human encounter—being godfather to a Maasai boy—I had found the last missing piece to the puzzle of myself. What did native Africans give me that white people could not? I imagine that those Maasai could as easily have been Brazilian Indians. What did count was that they were beings of Nature whose manner I found as soothing and exciting as the ways of the animals I studied. Of course, all the better was that the people of Maa, while as natural as the wildlife around us, were men and women with whom I could interact and with whom, by way of Sekerot or Sameri, I could communicate thoughts and emotions.

Once I had felt that I could never live where I did not speak the language of the locals, so I learned Spanish when I moved to Spain. But now, in middle age, I found the lack of direct communication not uncomfortable. Fortunately, Sameri was still too young to find constant translation boring. Besides, with it he seemed to achieve a certain status. Even though the orders were my own, he gave them to the men around camp, one a former warrior to whom all of his life he had bowed his head in respect, and I found it both amusing and attractive to hear my own thoughts expressed in his sweet voice and in words I could not understand. Sameri had the rare quality of always being at hand when I needed him, and seldom there when I wanted to be alone.

That Sameri was brave, as well as bright, could be seen from the half-dozen walnut-sized burn marks that scarred each of his thighs. These had come of self-inflicted wounds from embers placed on the skin, the custom practiced by both Maasai boys and girls, demonstrating a disdain for pain in preparation for the greater hurt of circumcision.

Having Sameri with me provided companionship, but also some worry. His senses were far keener than were mine. Giraffe on a ridge, which my naked eyes could not distinguish from saplings, were seen by him immediately. Once we stalked elephants, their number hidden by the heavy hillside shrubs and trees that we were approaching. Branches cracked, accompanied by the animals' satisfied rumblings and deep blowing.

"They are right there. Yes. In front. Yes." Sameri punctuated almost every phrase with "yes," as if to self-approve what he had just said. We crept closer. I scanned the cover for a raised trunk or the flap of an ear of the animals, which were now near enough for us to hear their stomachs gurgling. A side wind which had barely been in our favor changed course, noticed not only by us but by the elephants as they received our scent. Behind us and to either side, the ground stretched bare, void of cover for three hundred yards until the flat ended and a mountain of stone began. "Shall we go ahead?" I asked Sameri, whose true reply was read from his left foot placed sideways, ready to push off as he was about to turn in flight.

"No. They are very close. Yes," he answered.

That night, walking home, I felt his presence a liability. Anyone who has sat for hours in front of zoo lions or tigers will understand my concern. Half asleep and indifferent to the spectators who clap, shout, or whistle unsuccessfully to attract their attention, big cats, if a child passes, will leap to their feet, crouching, eyes fired and fixed on the small moving figure. Walking at dusk with Sameri sometimes made me uneasy. Once, as I watched him, barely visible in the evening gray, climb a bush to gather leleshwa leaves, I imagined the terror of a place like this with a man-eater prowling the fading light.

Sameri had climbed into the undergrowth to obtain deodorant, for at Ololasurai we turned to the bush to satisfy some hygenic needs. During a stroll, when my armpits started to reek, Sameri and I pulled leleshwa leaves to be slipped into my shirt and under my arms. By the time we arrived at camp, my body smelled of fresh camphor. Perhaps the leleshwa is the most important plant to the Maasai, its leaves serving not only as a deodorant, but for handkerchiefs, toilet paper, and bed padding, and its termite-resistant wood for arrows, clubs, building material, and fuel. Other trees provided dental hygiene. Each evening Moseka would cut a five-inch-long twig the diameter of a pencil from a greenheart tree to supply me with a fresh toothbrush. Once the tip of this bitter-tasting stick had been chewed and frayed, it could then be used to clean teeth and massage gums. Never, as in Ololasurai, have I felt my mouth so fresh as teeth, without the abrasive action of plastic bristles or pumice, became glassy smooth. Because one chewed on the stick, it was often kept in the mouth for fifteen or twenty minutes, polishing enamel and massaging gums. Maasai say that their white teeth alone distinguish them from other tribes. This, which can be confirmed in the portraits of this book, is the result not only of an almost exclusively calcium diet, but of the "wild toothbrush," several of which I tried to take back to Spain.

Occasionally night would find Sameri and me far from camp, high on one of the ridges which overlooked the flat of the valley, now dark except for dots of orange to indicate corrals and enkangs where people were bedding down their animals, preparing food, and soon readying themselves for sleep. Those fires were seen not only by us, but by any lion or leopard looking for an easy meal. Now the torch would be needed, both to show the way and, hopefully, to keep predators from our path. Sometimes, still three or four miles from the comfort and safety of the fire, we would stop at an enkang, where the plastic water bottle which Sameri carried would be filled with milk, as promised by someone who had passed the tent in early afternoon. While maize, some cabbage, occasional blood and meat are eaten by Maasai, milk, as I have said, is what they value most and consume daily, either in liquid form or curdled in yogurt.

Behind the thorn fence bobbed up the faces of women and children who could not believe that a white man accompanied by a slight child was standing out in the darkness while they huddled together around a fire in the safety of the thorn enclosure. The only white people most of them had seen had been from a distance, going and coming from the reserve; pale faces peering from behind the minivans' glass, like tropical fish in mobile aquariums. So, naturally, it was both unusual and amusing for them to see me through the thorn, and stranger yet to hear an "Olesere" from my lips before, as lions sounded, I disappeared into the blackness, a boy and a torch for protection.

Making our way toward camp, if the lions again announced their presence downstream or near the caves, I stopped to savor the noise much to Sameri's apprehensive amusement. Were I to hear it ten thousand times, never will I tire of a lion's roar or of the sight of a fever tree against the cobalt of approaching rain, each experienced as though for the first time.

As I have mentioned in my small friend's presence, animals were frequently sighted that I, alone, would not have seen. Occasionally, though, I did prove of slight value, for the binoculars gave me some advantage, and infrequently Sameri made mistakes both in what he saw and in his language. Once I spotted a lone eland high on a hill that his eyes took minutes to find. Another time, at dusk, he pointed to three dark shapes. "Buffalo," he whispered, warning me that I should look fast because one was moving into tall brush. Through the binoculars the shapes became their reality— three olive trees. Another time, "Look, look!" he said, pointing upward. "It is there. It is there. Yes." Accustomed to his acute young Maasai eyes and their ability to sight objects that to me did not exist, I swung the binoculars in an arc across the sky.

"Where is it? Where?" I questioned.

"There! There!" he pointed patiently, but with animation. "There are two of them. Yes. Two angels!"

I squinted more intently into the binoculars. "Angels?" I asked.

"I mean eagles," he giggled.

Sometimes, as we quickened our pace toward home, a thought would cross my mind, and aware that it would escape if not jotted down at the moment, I would pause in the darkness and take out pen and ragged notebook. The quivering beam of Sameri's torch illuminated the page, while his apprehensive eyes searched the darkness for the danger that his imagination and experience placed in the night.

Once Sekerot and Miton were off to Narok and Loita for a wedding that would keep them away for days. The time was not lonely, as I had expected, but was as attractive, in another way, as when my friends were present. Camp life slowed in pace. There was less activity, fewer intrusions by human voices, while those of animals and birds seemed more prominent. I took advantage of the time to write, except when, with the excuse of Maasai visitors, I retired with them to the shade in an exchange of questions translated by Sameri, mine about Cape buffalo, Maasai tradition and life, theirs about places beyond Kenya and the jumbo 747 that sounded over Ololasurai every night at nine sharp. My friends' absence also meant not only that I was earlier to bed, but that I felt freer in staying out later on afternoon walks, something of which Sekerot would have disapproved.

After returning to camp in the darkness, I would have

my meal at the campfire with men who sang songs of a pitch and rhythm that were strange to my ears. However, these repeated chants were vaguely reminiscent of those voiced by Indians in the cowboy films that we had watched as boys at the Alex Theatre matinees in Glendale. Here, at Ololasurai, the figures that hunched around me were likewise hooded in brightly colored blankets which gave comfort from the night chill, while, behind us, pointed spear handles stuck into the ground, their blades glistening sharply toward the moon. In those moments I felt fortunate in a strange way to faintly realize a North American fantasy, which before this time in Africa would have seemed impossible.

These people were called Maasai, not Sioux, Crow, or Cherokee, but like those American natives, my African friends were men of nature. By being the only whiteness in their presence at Ololasurai, I was privileged with a glimpse into a natural past way of life similar to that of my own country and of the "noble savages" who had inhabited it. Below, on the plain, masses of wildebeest, as great in their number as the vast buffalo herds that once roamed the American West, could haze the sun and bring thunder to the midday brightness. Here homes were also made of natural material to form one with the landscape. They were not constructed of animal skins or called teepees, but fashioned of cow dung and by some marvelous bit of luck, their doorways were open to me.

Another time, when Sekerot was off to Narok, not to return until midnight, I was wakened from an early sleep by the death cries of a zebra. They came from somewhere across the far stream where I almost daily hunted butterflies. This disturbing sound was followed by the rumble of hooves belonging to the herd from which the lion had chosen his prey. On a windy night, this noise would not

have broken my sleep, but would have been muffled by the incessant blow and lashing of the tent. However, there were also windless nights when no calls came from hyenas, lions, zebra, or leopards, when only a cricket rubbed together its wings to remind us that we were alive and could still hear.

At breakfast the next morning, before leaving camp, Moseka told of hearing the lions approaching down the valley from the caves. Then had come the anguished screams of the zebra. By midday the camp was empty, except for Masiene scrubbing clothes and me at the typewriter, where I had been sitting long enough to justify getting up for a break. The sun had warmed the wings of butterflies, who now glided en masse across the meadow toward the far stream and the leached minerals and moisture that it promised. Taking the net, I walked the clearing toward the stream crossing, thinking of the screams in the night and Sekerot's warning before he had left camp early that morning: No one should approach the area of the zebra kill until Moseka had returned and could take time to see if the lions had moved on or had lain up in thick cover near the water.

As I neared the place where I caught butterflies and where last night the lion had captured a zebra, I moved slowly down the steep trail that cut through high bush. The only bird cries came from far away. As I approached the water, I did not see or hear anything to distinguish the quiet scene before me from that which I had experienced countless times when treading this same muddied buffalo path. Where water met sand, big cat footprints stamped into the smoothness of the far shore caught my eye just as the heavy flapping of wings startled my heart. Two white-backed vultures lit in branches thirty feet overhead and, not having seen me, craned their necks, peering into the undergrowth directly across the bank. Taking care of the placement of my feet on the muddy shore, I began to move backward. With lions and their strong ideas of possession, I had had some experience. A leaf, a spot of grass, and, more obvious, a bone or piece of meat, once claimed by a lion as his own, may be defended until death. On the other hand, an entire pride can be sent bounding from a kill by a person who, outside of their flight zone, runs forward waving his arms. This, however, is not always the case. I once saw a film of a German tourist who got out of a car while filming a pride of lions on a buffalo kill thirty feet away. As the German stepped forward, photographed by another tourist in a Land-Rover, the lions lunged, knocked him down, and ate him in front of the car which held his hysterical wife and children.

Slight white lines still scar the back of my left hand, cut there by a lion cub I called by name, one who had sat on my lap before the fireplace in Spain. Mistakenly, I had tried to take from him something that his small mind was not able to concede. If the cover around me now was dense enough to conceal an elephant at twenty yards, what were one's chances of locating anything smaller? The cub in Spain had been one thing. A full-grown lion at Ololasurai defending a zebra kill would be another matter. The vultures stared with more intensity toward the ground. What could their eyes see that mine could not? A mesh of stripes, black and white hair split over bloodied ribs? Or did they see nothing at all?

Back at the tent, with the binoculars, Masiene and I watched the vultures until we had almost grown tired of speculating about their behavior, at which time they hopped into lower branches and out of view. Later that afternoon, when Moseka returned, he and I walked up-stream and slowly crisscrossed the bank from one side to the other before exploring a slight meadow wedged into the far hillside. We found no drag marks, no splinters of bone, not a trace of white or black hair or a fleck of blood on the new grass. That the zebra had died somewhere within several hundred yards from us and that lions had made the kill could hardly be questioned. What happened after that, we would never know.

At Ololasurai, as in most of nature, the majority of predator attacks were unsuccessful. Stalks were repeated again and again before food was secured. Late one afternoon, soaping myself, concealed by the shower's leaf curtain, which also served as a blind, I spied a flock of feeding, helmeted guineafowl twenty-five yards away. Suddenly, amid screams and scattering, the guineas took flight as a martial eagle burst in among them. Feathers seemed to explode as the eagle bowled over one of the screeching birds, which somehow escaped to take cover under a bush. Like a hound after a hare the eagle circled the shrub in awkward steps, not willing to give up his almost-meal. But the guinea, surprisingly, did not panic, as had the rest of the flock, now high on the hill behind the tent, screeching warnings or encouragement—one could not be sure which. Finally, in an admission of defeat, the eagle rose into the air and glided to the twisted top of a charred olive tree. There, he waited for some time, as did I in the shower. But there was no movement in the clearing except for a cluster of white polka-dotted charcoal feathers that were spun, lifted, and spread by the wind.

My afternoon walks most often were taken along the streams, in one of several directions, or into the low hills where patches of thick forest provided cover to whatever creatures my imagination wished to place there (and which at one time or another actually were there). At the beginning of my stay, I was so apprehensive on these outings that dry leaves moved by a sudden breeze were enough to startled me. But experience and my Maasai friends taught me that if one does not "let blood sleep," the bush was far less dangerous than were our infrequent journeys in Miton's Land-Rover, which sometimes left the ground at kamikaze speed and determination, its treadless tires spinning freely, while the entire contraption, held together by baling wire and pieces of wood, seemed on the verge of momentary disintegration. Whether the brakes worked or not was a continuing uncertainty. Once, roaring down the Supuko escarpment from Loita, only Miton's stony calm restrained me from flinging open the door and leaping to any other fate but the certain death which remaining in the car seemed to signify.

Apart from Sameri, when he was at Ololasurai and I was in the mood for his company, my companion on some of these walks was Chui, a yellow cur that protected the sheep at the upstream enkang and who had taken a liking to our camp, probably more for the tidbits we tossed him than for our affectionate pats on his head. Chui seemed to me unusually secure with people, for, as loving as most Maasai can be with their hoofed domestics, they could be unkind to dogs whose mere presence frequently called for a stoning. This was a point of disagreement between me and Sekerot, who argued that many Maasai love their dogs and treat them with affection. As an example of this, he told the story of Simba, a mutt who, while accompanying warriors during a lion hunt, bravely risked his neck to hold the beast at bay while the moran speared it to death. Then a hero, the dog was carried back to the enkang and paraded around it on the warriors' shoulders.

While Simba had been named (in Swahili) for the lion which he had defied, Chui was inexplicably named after the leopard, which above all other meat favors that of dog. "Kuyia" (when pronounced, it sounds like "queer") is the name to which most Maasai dogs respond. Why Chui had been given his seemingly incongruous handle, we were never told. What was sure, however, was that he barely seemed to tolerate us when, without his consent, we tried to make him a camp pet. Sekerot even carried him into the shower and, with my jojoba shampoo, scrubbed him so that later, when dry in the sun, his yellow fur was full and fluffy.

Night after night, when we were in bed and the fire no more than a trace of orange, Chui would jump camp and dash through the darkness to his enkang home a half mile upstream. Why he did this, not even his real owners could understand. But I always felt the call of duty, protecting sheep and lambs, drew him back to the thorn enclosure. Anyone who knows about leopards and dogs will find it unbelievable that this yellow flash in the blackness repeated his seemingly suicidal run for thirty-one nights, returning to the tent each morning to hear us praise his daring while we tossed him tributes of scraps.

In the end, it was not a leopard, but an immature lion that ended both our pet's nighttime sojourns and his life. When the lion jumped the thorn to kill a calf, all the other watchdogs had cowered but Chui, who had charged forward in a gesture of bravado only to have his brave heart torn from his freshly scrubbed yellow chest.

The next morning, when Chui's owner came to camp to give us the bad news and to sharpen his spear, the only words of solace we could offer were: "Better a dead brave dog than a live scorned coward like the rest." Chui had lived as he had died, while daring greatly. When leopards or lions killed a dog or livestock, herdsmen came to the tent not only to tell us of the tragic happenings, but, in preparation for the next attack, to sharpen their spears with our file. Some also brought injured or sick sheep or goats, and occasionally when those we treated survived, the owner would later come back to the tent with the healthy animal in hand. We had returned it to life, so now it was returned to us in appreciation of our "kindness and caring." Such is the Maasai way.

When Chui was alive, his presence on my walks had its price. Though he could detect creatures out of sight and at great distance, his frequently impatient company alerted birds and animals which would have remained unaware of my stony presence. Sometimes, alone, distant from camp, I strolled slowly, now and then pausing to scan the hills and vegetation for movement. Occasionally I walked faster and farther until I arrived at a boulder or fallen tree that promised good vantage. There I would sit, elbows resting on drawn-up knees to steady the binoculars, remaining as stationary as possible until the failing light beckoned me back to camp. Bird alarms were of more help than the field glasses in locating a stalking or crouching predator. Francolins, helmeted guineafowl and bare-headed go-away birds, as well as the smaller hornbills, were invaluable in detecting the movement of leopards. The "ummmmmmmmm-pooooo" of vervet monkeys, accompanied by exaggerated movements of their heads, was also useful, as were the short, gruff, serious alarms voiced by baboons. More than once a bushbuck in thick green cover along the stream barked to make me aware of a leopard's presence. Startled yaps of zebra and the brash exaltations of impala were voiced with such frequency that only occasionally were they of use in locating cats, big or small. Superb starlings and weaverbirds had our thanks for announcing the presence of snakes. At dusk, I spent hours watching helmeted guineafowl foraging side by side with baboons and impala, all of which enjoyed the relative security of the collective warning system. The bird's long legs and bright blue heads appeared streamlined in comparison to those of the closely related pale-faced domestic variety whose shorter legs and coarse bodies have been selectively bred, degenerated from the wild, to suit the gastronomic whims of man.

Sometimes, near the caves, a bush would sway as if by the breeze or a twig would crack. At times I was uncertain of my company and often thought I might have been spied on by the Ndorobo hunters who occasionally made their home in the holes of rock above the path. Scurrying about with loads of honey, hides, meat, leather straps, bows, poisoned arrows, and clubs while dressed in dull rags, these little men move as silently as dust on the wind. The Maasai say that the Ndorobo dash so rapidly that the friction of their feet on the ground leaves behind trails of smoke. True men of the bush, the Ndorobo are frequently less detectable to outsiders than the wild animals they stalk. When carrying honey, if Ndorobo notice the presence of strangers, they flee, not only leaving behind the fruit of their gathering but the question: Was there really something there, or was it my imagination? Much as the Ndorobo attempt to mimic Maasai, Sekerot told me, the result is totally unsuccessful. Ndorobo say that the buffalo are their cattle and zebra their donkeys, and in this way they are like Maasai. However, they kill their "livestock" instead of nurturing them, which the people of Maa find deplorable.

Maasai feel that the Ndorobo lack not only feeling for animals but pride; nevertheless, they are respected as hunters, tanners, honey gatherers, blacksmiths, and circumcisers. No one forgets that they play the paramount role in converting a Maasai youth into a man. Though the Ndorobo have their own tongue, they also speak the language of the Maasai, of whom they are apprehensive. Sekerot told me that if Ndorobo could not be identified by manner of speech or dress, Maasai could distinguish their strong body odor, which is said to come from eating animal fat, especially that of zebra. "Ndorobo" (or "Dorobo") is derived from the Maa *ol toroboni*, meaning "poor folk," because they do not own cattle and are reduced to eating the meat of wild animals.

Occasionally on my walks I would seek cover beneath a stunted tree or in heavy brush, concealed from the eyes of the animals and birds that, unconscious of my presence, attended to their lives without concern. Once at dusk I was sitting as still as a stone in the open when slight movement over my right shoulder became a female hyena and two furry pups passing downwind not more than twenty feet away. Disappointingly, they were not the leopard which was the object of that vigil. This animal, who nightly stole sheep and goats from the corrals up- and downstream, and who had kept our dog's life hanging from the slimmest thread, also caused us to lose an entire grocery supply. Lepish, loaded with heavy sacks of provisions, returning from market six miles away, climbed a mountain of rock to come face to face with the leopard, the sight of which sent him plummeting backward, tumbling down that steep stony hillside, potatoes, sugar, cabbage, onions, maize, flour, tea, cooking oil, and fruit scattered almost beyond recovery.

When Sekerot was away, I stayed later and strayed

farther than my walks should have taken me. Usually, as darkness fell and I neared camp, a figure would appear—Moseka—whose fine features would be indistinguishable in the approaching darkness. He would then walk behind, hurrying me along like a herdsman urging forward cattle that had been lost or strayed and, in the going light, risked not returning at all. With him, blanket hooding his head and body, I would sometimes sit up late at the fire and he would begin to sing in a high falsetto boy's voice, punctuated with heavy warrior breathing, grunts and growls that welled up from the depths of his diaphragm, lungs, throat, and soul. As his head undulated back and forth he seemed not in Ololasurai at all, but lost in the happiest days of his life, those of the moran. Moseka's voice in the flickering darkness was as pleasing to the ear as was the cracking campfire and night sounds that accompanied it. Sitting around the dying embers with men whose language I did not speak or understand was not uncomfortable, for their presence alone provided comfort and fraternity.

"We should go for buffalo again and spend the night near the salt licks and marsh," said Sekerot late one afternoon. "And we will carry the one-man tent." In a half hour the horses were saddled and packed and we were on our way. Where the stream widened and low hills on either side opened to form a seemingly endless valley, we encountered a trio of immature giraffe, which, from a distance, watched disinterestedly as we trotted the mares along with Morkau leading on foot, his spear held high. Narok and Katie quickened their gait without the touch of our heels, when in the forest above the valley a branch cracked, followed by the deep rumbling and blowing of elephants. We guided the horses toward a marsh that on one side was bordered with a stream walled high by a white chalky embankment which animals, wild and domestic, had pitted deeply in search of salt.

With the approach of evening, a fine drizzle forced us inside the confines of the tent and almost extinguished our fire, which sparkled weakly in the horses' eyes. They would not spend tonight in the security of the corral, but in the open, where only Morkau's spear and torch could protect them from whatever lurked out in the damp darkness. Hooded in a soggy blanket, Morkau stood guard, while Sekerot and I half slept. At five in the morning, I unzipped the tent flap and crawled out into the foggy pitch. The rain had stopped, and to warm myself I half hung against the black mare's side, listening to her steady respiration while myself breathing the sweetness of horses nourished on fresh grass. When first light showed the way, I walked along a hill above the marsh and, with the binoculars, searched the high reeds for Cape buffalo.

Before the sun had risen, Sekerot and I had left Morkau with the horses and set off on foot, passing through meadows of dewy grass fringed with thornbush, which after several miles narrowed, closing in on the path we had chosen. Where on other rides or walks here, zebra, impala, and topi had abounded, this morning, there was little movement or sound except for birds, whose voices and damp wings were rising with the gray dawn.

Then came the pungent odor of buffalo, as a hundred yards ahead, in a narrow corridor, back-lit vapor rose from piles of hot dung fuming in the early morning coolness. We moved slowly through a maze of thorn, and with each step the heavy smell of buffalo sweat overpowered scents of which moments before we had been aware. As we controlled breathing so as not to muffle our hearing and fanned hands out, cupped behind our ears, to net the snap of a twig or sigh of a buffalo, there came another sound from not more than a stone's throw away as a lion growled lowly in annoyance. I turned my head slowly toward Sekerot. "Do you want to continue?"

"Do you?" he returned the question.

"Until those rocks." I gestured toward a pile of boulders that bulged from the thorn thirty feet ahead and to the right of where the growls had menaced. We climbed the cold roundness of stone and waited, still governing our breathing while scanning the lattice of thorn for a glimpse of a tawny coat, the flicker of a black-tipped ear, or the momentary glisten of buffalo horn tips or boss. Were the animals searched for by our ears and eyes quietly watching us? Several weaver birds winged like gulls over the sea of gray in flashes that showed their plumage to be eclipsing from nondescript to canary yellow and black. After a half hour, we slid to the wet earth and trod back to Morkau and the horses.

Overhead the sun soon burned down with the intensity that clear sky projects in advance of the fall of rain. Here on the equator, the red of the earth seemed redder, the green of acacia tops greener, as if the sun's purity distilled those colors to their very essence. Between the black mare's ears stretched as far as one's vision could discern a ribbon of fever trees, whose reach into the sky showed they had long been reflected in the shallow current of Olmerrui, "the never contaminated river." From near Oloosekisekin Hill the Olmerrui flowed to the Mara before emptying into Lake Victoria. Even the slight stream which passed within sixty yards of our tent and which joined the Olmerrui, contributed to the Nile's flow. In the filtered shade of this narrow forest, elephants in considerable number stomped the mud and sprayed their backs silver with Olmerrui's freshness.

Sekerot's enkang commanded a splendid view of the river as it stretched, seemingly shaded from one end of the valley to the other by the twisted boughs of lime that triangled up to open wide supporting stratum after stratum of the fever trees' delicate, dark-green foliage. Passing Sekerot's mother's house and that of his stepmother, we were joined by tunicked or naked children. Those who knew the horses approached reverently with bowed heads, waiting for us to lean from the saddles and touch our fingers to the shiny, smoothly shaven blackness of their scalps. Without hesitating longer, we rode on until, from a rise that was spiked and adorned with the sword leaves and red blossoms of aloe plants, we gazed out across a plain to distant mountains veiled in mauve.

"I can remember," said Sekerot as he leaned back and rested his hand on the roundness of the mare's chestnut flank, "looking out and seeing elephants from here to there." He pointed toward the trace of mountain in the distance. "See that forest to the right? It is called 'the place that flesh fears.' Yesterday lions killed a buffalo in front of those thorn trees."

Late that afternoon we again approached Sekerot's enkang, where he paused to visit his grandmother. As in all Maasai dwellings, the almost total darkness of the hut was heavy with smoke, and it took the eyes moments to stop watering and distinguish forms. A dim torch was turned on so that I could see the grandmother's wrinkles, smile, and cataract-clouded eyes, as well as the details of her home. We sat on a berth stretched tight with hard, stiff hide, and as my friend and the mother of his dead father exchanged tender sounds of affection, I leaned back on the bed, entranced by rays of smoky light that from several hardly-there-at-all holes in the ceiling or wall pierced the darkness. Even the most sophisticated laser

show could not rival the delicate razor-sharp beams that cut through the smoky blackness.

Sleep almost overtook me, lulled by the soft, drawn-out ayyyyyyyyyyyyyyes and oooooooohhhhhhs and eeehhhhhhhhhs that were exchanged between my friend and his grandmother, a sweet contrast to the accents of Spain where it seems that everyone shouts and talks at once while listening to no one. How different was this, where I lay in the blackness, from anything my being had previously experienced: here where weeks ago the Maasai body odor or sweat and the smoke absorbed by it was disgusting to my nose, now my own armpits reeked of the same acrid scent; here men, women, and children cleared their lungs and noses to spit with gusto wherever they might be; here occasionally before a handshake saliva was blown on the palm in a gesture of favor; here single and married men unjealously shared their girlfriends and wives with age-mates; here heterosexual men and youths walked hand in hand, fingers interlaced; here girls before adolescence are famous among warriors for techniques of lovemaking; here an act of cowardice hangs around the shamed one's neck until jackals are gnawing at his bones; here any adult can take the cane to any misbehaving child; here the word "why" never crosses the mind of a child told by an adult to carry out a task; here all children bow their heads respectfully to receive an adult's condescending touch; here, regardless of how bright or brave a boy is, he is never thought of as "a little man" or equal but treated and loved as a child; here given first names are never used by fathers to their sons or between best friends who employ pet names for one another; here politeness and respect are as important today as they were hundreds of years ago; here every minute behavior has a rule from which variation is unthinkable; here at a remote manyata somewhere in the Loita Hills on the Tanzanian border I could be the only white face among several thousand black ones whose eyes met mine with little more than curiosity and indifference; here I would be called by my friend, but no one else, a name which before my ears had never known, Inkirragat ("my campfire companion"); here cattle are more valuable than diamonds or gold, and cows obey their owners as do domestic dogs; here fresh cow dung is no more distasteful to the hand or bare foot than would be clean-washed beach sand; here the people are not so presumptuous and shallow as to worship and portray God in their image and give Him a common first name (Engai, in Maa, means God and encompasses all of the forces and subtleties of nature, in dimensions that most "civilized" religions cannot conceive); here, when a man expires, friends and family abandon the dead body as if it were an empty discarded cardboard carton (they mourn the lost spirit, but never again pronounce the deceased person's name); here man lives in harmony with nature, surrounded by the earth's most exotic wildlife—the trophy hunter's Valhalla, home of the "big five"—and yet rarely kills except for ceremonial reasons or in defense of self and property; and here the sounds of whistling herd boys, piping doves, and lowing cattle are sweeter to the ear than the glitzy beat that announces the six o'clock news and the violence and tragedy reported on it.

Then came my last day at Ololasurai. The morning sun dazzled the finery and thorns of the twisted fever-tree branches above the rainfly. Two tropical boubous chorused, bobbing on twigs that arched the stream while intermittently rasping the air with electrical sounds. Doves cooed from all directions. An oriole warbled with the breeze upon which a tawny eagle sailed to its nest on the flatness of an umbrella acacia behind the tent. A zebra barked in the direction of the caves. Far on the other side of the stream goat bells chimed the air. The brilliant green leaves that five weeks ago had been carefully placed to screen the shower were now faded or dead, almost as if to indicate a change in season.

Somewhere behind the tent, Moseka and Morkau sang softly, then appeared, spears in hand, to stop and gaze across the pasture where the chestnut mare was grazing. The Maasai youths stood silently, stork-like, with one foot propped against the other leg's calf. The breeze that brushed their bronzed-chocolate foreheads passed through long-stretched pierced earlobes decorated with beads as colorful as were the butterflies that glided about the distant figure of the mare. Morkau's face was still gaunt from the anthrax which recently had almost ended his life.

Toga-like shukas fluttered to expose solid buttocks, sinewy loins, and long slim calves. Under the sun, shoulder muscles glistened and slightly rippled like water over rounded-smooth stream stones. The youths remained silent in front of the tent, eyes fixed on the strange animal they had grown to love and call by name. Moseka and Morkau were much more of yesterday than of today, the remnants of a dying race. They were testimony to a people whose traditions have defied many of the superficial material and religious seductions of a so-called modern world. Most of their friends wore plastic digital watches, and before long others would be transported by Walkman from Maasailand and the grazing cattle in their charge to faraway, antiseptic places of cement, frenzied confusion, steel, and glass, where the words "family," "respect," and "honor" have long been burned in smoldering garbage dumps which gray the once-blue sky overhead.

The blue over the tent was crossed by a minute, white jet stream, an aircraft that in minutes would leave below the Maasai settlements, that even from lower altitude were barely distinguishable from the natural landscape. Before long, the plane would be passing over hazy cities which, from the air, would appear like blight on a once lovely piece of fruit. Soon I would be on such a plane. Rising from the canvas chair, I walked to Moseka and Morkau and with them enjoyed, for what seemed the last time—maybe ever—the morning view from the tent.

At the end of that day, as I returned from my final walk into the hills, the sky darkened with such rapidity and I had stayed out so long and unsafely late that as I finally saw the orange of the campfire, a concerned Sekerot was dispatching Morkau and Sicona, torches and spears in hand, to search for me.

That last walk had taken me up the valley toward the caves which Sekerot seemed to enjoy, but which I found uninviting, even though their stones were of the richest rusts and ochers, feathered with lime-green fronds and delicate wildflowers. Inside one of them were two Maasai shields, as dull and aged in their finish as was the dust and ash in which they lay. Sekerot thought they were maybe one hundred years old, he was not sure. But he was certain that all Maasai, himself included, respected—as part of the cave—those two stretched-tough pieces of buffalo hide, as well as the memory of the warriors who had made and used them.

Drops of rain fell lightly. Otherwise, stillness prevailed. Not even a jackal or dik-dik bolted across the hoof-etched zebra trail that I followed. Far up the valley, I chanced upon a herd of resident impala, whose buck ripped and tore the air with short exaltations of alarm before bounding off, harem in pursuit. Where were the zebra whose almost constant presence was written on the path upon which I walked? The rusty flash of a paradise flycatcher was the only sign of birdlife, where, on the other outings, the air had vibrated with wings and song. I sat down on an ant mound and, with the binoculars, searched the hillsides and trees. There was no trace of movement where, on other walks, life had teemed. However, this was simply Africa. One moment the black cotton soil was dry, rock-hard and resounding underfoot. Seconds later it would rain and our boots would make noisy slurps as we plodded through the mud.

How long would it be, I wondered, before I would return here, if I returned at all? Living a choice life is frequently given little importance until it ends, and my days at Ololasurai had so passed until these last moments of reflection. The sound of a Maasai walking stick tapping stone brought me from those thoughts, as a lone figure, the red of his blanket practically lost in the darkness, a minute being against the blue of the hillside, was racing night to reach his enkang upstream.

With great effort, I rose from the ant mound. Cumulus rolled from behind the hill above the caves and, through the binoculars, appeared to boil like surf, dark under light, light under dark, great billows cascading over one another, rimmed with platinum by the setting sun as the clouds crossed each other in endless layers. One shaft of sunlight silhouetted a lone vulture, gliding the last moments of day. In the profound stillness, except for the acacia trees and plant life, there was little to distinguish Ololasurai from other places I had known.

As I walked toward camp, the leader of a baboon troop, balanced in the highest reaches of a fig tree, jumped up and down on a limb, the far end of which held two hysterical youngsters clinging to slender twigs and leaves. As the enraged adult shook the branch with more determination, the young baboons, screaming for their lives, lost grip and, like a pair of fallen aerialists, plummeted a hundred feet down into a network of thick shrubbery. A smile drew my lips and winged out the wrinkles that fanned the outer edges of my eyes.

As I neared camp, where Sekerot, Sicona, and Morkau watched my approach, tropical boubous dueted twice and were silent.

POSTSCRIPT—
Ololasurai,
August 10, 1990

A year has passed, and between then and now are names that mean little to me— Madrid, Los Angeles, London, New York— as I again sit in front of the tent, before which ocher remnants of last summer's grass rise sparsely in defiance of fire. The ash, against which they stand, is a fortnight old.

When I arrived from Nairobi yesterday afternoon, it rained. And, as I took shelter in the tent, I was joined by an uninvited Maasai, a neglected, retarded boy who had been brought to camp by his older brother's kindness. As the rain pounded the tent, the boy's smoked and rancid body odors took possession of our canvas refuge. For a while he lay curled against my sleeping bag, quivering with cold, staring at nothing. Where the being was behind those innocent eyes, no one will ever know, no more than the brain that focused them.

The boy, it was clear, had never been so close to a white man. Uninhibited, he finally reached out to un-ashamedly touch my short, silky—to his rough hand— hair, and a smile brightened the darkness of the tent. Again he passed his hand over my scalp. Then, with crusted, black, filthy fingers he caressed the paleness of my cheek, at which his grin widened. Seeing that I did not restrict his curiosity, he drew near to sniff the soap odor of the freshly scrubbed khaki shirt. At the scent, his nose wrinkled with displeasure. Cast back a century in time, a similar first encounter with a white man had preluded the undoing of his race.

Rain ceased pattering the green canvas fly above the tent, which I now unzipped, and the boy was gone, except for his stench, which lingered until the next morning. Looking at the dark sky behind the tent, I saw a pair of tawny eagles, clearly the same ones from last year, roost-ing at the pinnacle of the dead acacia's center spire. They had returned to Ololasurai, and so had I.

ACKNOWLEDGMENTS

First to be thanked are my parents. My father taught us about loving nature and how to study it. My mother taught us that even a boy from the wrong side of the tracks in Glendale could one day live among the Maasai, if that was his dream.

My friend Mary Daniels was more help with this project than she will ever realize. She read and—reread—the manuscript while offering suggestions that will contribute to any success this book might have.

Bill Wheeler not only arranged my first trip to Africa but later introduced me to Sekerot Ole Mpetti, who made the adventure in Kenya possible. Sekerot would not have been able to come to America, where I met him, had it not been for the help of Bill and Linda Wheeler, Colleen Quinn, Mr. and Mrs. Reginald K. Brack, Jr., Leni Goldsmith, Onke and James Wilde, and Dominic and Kathyrine Embrossio.

In Kenya I would again like to thank Dr. Alberto Bencivenga as well as Bill and Liz McGill for their assistance and compassion in those difficult hours and days following Joe's buffalo injury.

Michel Van Steene is a Frenchman enamored of Kenya, its wildlife and people. He has spent years in that country and I hope one day he will write a book about his unique experience. Michel not only offered me his hospitality during each of my stays in Nairobi, but took time to read my manuscript and to offer valuable and astute suggestions. More important, without his long friendship with Sekerot, this book would most certainly never have been done.

For his presence at Ololasurai, I thank Miton Ole Siloma, who not only provided transportation when we needed it but, more important, gave me his friendship. For helping to keep the Land-Rover running and for his assistance around camp, I thank Exhaust. I also deeply thank the Maasai friends who took care of our camp: Sicona, Morkau, Lepish, Moseka, and Masiene. Also to be thanked for helping with our transportation are Sikindi and Sujinda Dhillon. Jean Marie Sabin and Nick Wood offered us their assistance and advice as did Tamsin Corcoran.

In Nairobi I thank Kay Turner for talking to me about her late husband and his interest in Cape buffalo and bullfighting.

There would not have been a tent at Ololasurai had it not been first for Bill Wheeler who provided it and for Mike Bates who generously brought it with him to Kenya. David Kader again also helped with outfitting our safari.

Once more Rick Fabares proved that he is as good a friend as he is a talented artist. As laboratory associate, his creative sensitivity and indefatigble devotion to this project will play a major part in any success that it may enjoy.

Manila Clough, who for years I have known and encouraged as an artist, has my deepest gratitude for her concern and friendship during the duration of this project.

To Mike Scanlon and Award Prints of San Diego, appreciation is expressed for the care they took with my work.

For the hours spent typing my manuscript, I thank Sally Stein and Julie Ebsen.

While designing this book, I again counted on the good advice of Barbara Chance.

Jay Vavra and Kelli Wong have my gratitude for the long hours they devoted to helping me with the layout of these pages.

John Dixon I thank for his help with the single-tone illustrations that appear in the last eighty pages of this book.

For his help with the calligraphy for the dust jacket, I am grateful to John Fulton for again providing me with good advice.

Jim Brown I thank for reading the manuscript and for his suggestions.

Bill Toone and Sunni Black I thank for providing me with a net that caught most of the butterflies that rest on these pages.

Chromacolor has my appreciation for the job they did processing my film which was Ektachrome 400 pushed to 800ASA.

At William Morrow and Company I first thank Al Marchioni, along with Larry Hughes, Lela Rolontz, and my friend and editor Andy Ambraziejus, for their continued support. Gloria Loomis, my agent, also has my deepest gratitude for her help and encouragement.

In Germany I thank Rudolf Blanckenstein for his guidance and association with this project. For keeping things going in Spain, I am grateful to José Franco. There I also thank the Nordmann family for their long-time support. In Sevilla, Miguel Angel Pinto has my gratitude for his help with my film.

In Barcelona I thank Cayfosa and Guillermo Mateu for doing such a fine job printing these pages.

Ron and Gale Vavra I thank for supplying me with film and for taking care of me during the final work on this book.

Kizzy I thank for her African presence.

GLOSSARY

boma	Swahili word for corral
eliyio	loneliness
enkang	a permanent Maasai settlement used by families, composed of a circular corral incorporating domed huts made of cow dung into its fence of thorn
inkirragat	my campfire companion
inkera oo motonyi	children of the birds
manyata	also spelled *manyatta*. A temporary Maasai settlement used for special ceremonies
miraa	or *khat*, a narcotic drug well known to Arabs and Somalis
Ndorobo	an East African tribe of hunters. The word is derived from the Maa *ol toroboni*, meaning poor folk who do not own any cattle and are reduced to eating the meat of wild animals. *Endorobo* in Maa means tsetse fly.
olesere	good-bye
ol ashumpai	originally meaning an Arab; hence the Maasai still call a white man *ol ashumpai oilbor*: the white Arab.
ol chore	my friend
ol chorelai	my special friend
ol kaporri	meaning white man but with a derogatory connotation.
ol musungui	or *ol musunkui*, derived from the Swahili *mzungu*, meaning white man, European.
shuka	Swahili for the piece of calico worn as a loincloth or toga (in Maa: *ol karasha*)
supa	hello

BUTTERFLIES, FEATHERS, AND PRESSED PLANTS

Most of the butterflies, feathers, and pressed plants that appear in the color section of this book were gathered at Ololasurai or while on safari into the Loita Hills.